WAKE UP WORLD!

Apocalypse Cometh Prophecy

BOOK TWO

LEW OSTEEN

WAKE UP WORLD!:
Apocalypse Cometh Prophecy
Copyright © 2023 **Lew Osteen**

ISBN (Paperback): 978-1-958475-39-3
ISBN (Hardback): 978-1-958475-40-9
ISBN (Ebook): 978-1-958475-41-6

Because of the dynamic nature of the Internet, any web addresses or links contained in this book may have changed since publication and may no longer be valid. The views expressed in the work are solely those of the author and do not necessarily reflect the views of the publisher, and the publisher hereby disclaims any responsibility for them.

Printed in the United States of America.

PROMINENT
BOOKS

5830 E 2nd St, Ste 7000 #9983
Casper, WY 82609
USA

CHAPTER ONE

Michael watched as John approached the building's edge and looked down to the street 66 floors below. John did not seem afraid, and Michael knew he might take the leap of faith at any moment. Michael also knew he was close to being rebellious in helping Sam and John. Yet he saw that Lucifer had seduced the world into an evil slumber with few righteous people left. If Satan could turn the 144,000 god-fearing people remaining away from God, then perhaps he could save himself.

Michael thought of descending to earth and striking the sinful with the Sword of the Word to wake them up to the evil about them.

But he dismissed that thought as foolish and dangerous.

He knew the bottomless, fiery pit could hold more than one.

*   *   *

The weak sunrise could not penetrate the dark toxic fog that enveloped the streets of San Francisco, where Sam now stood alone in the fog. Malcolm had kept his word and sent a Luxury Limo to bring him to The City. Sam had made the driver ditch the women and the liquor and was a little surprised he had arrived here safe. As the fog closed in around him, he wondered if he was lost in some weird dream.

When he saw the Golden Calf logo of Malcolm's Headquarters, he knew it was no dream. His hand went to his neck and felt for the necklace. He cursed himself for his lack of faith and vowed to never think of it again.

The fog was so thick that when Sam stood and looked up toward the rooftop, he could see only three floors up, so he had no idea if John was still being forced to stand on the edge. He hoped John had enough common sense to deny God and save his life. Of course, that would not guarantee anything with the deceitful Malcolm, but it would be better than falling 66 stories to your death.

Sam looked at the front door entrance and noticed it was unguarded. He chuckled at Malcolm's obvious ruse to get in inside where he would be at Malcolm's mercy. His ankle was much better, so, Sam had decided the only safe way into Malcolm's lair was to climb up the backside of the building where he knew of a security blind spot. He had climbed the 3000-foot-tall El Capitan countless times and knew where he could get good footholds. All he had here were the Window Washer's stanchions and a good rope. It was insane to try, but what Malcolm was doing to Ahwahnee, John, and most of the world was more insane and had to be ended.

Sam's thoughts went to Tiye. He figured leaving the note and the necklace were done on orders from Malcolm. It hurt to think of her and "Donavan" together and he did not know if he could kill her on sight. He knew she thought he was crazy and climbing 66 stories in the fog would only confirm that notion. It was crazy, but he hoped, slim as his chances were, the fog and the element of surprise just might help him succeed.

The towering, black stone edifice seemed to mock him as he wondered if maybe this was not a good idea. Sam knew he had a dark side, and day by day, The Black Dog was taking him deeper into his private hell. He knew he wasn't out to save the world, so much as guilt over his denial of his people and leaving his mother to die alone.

He knew deep inside it was all of them. Yet this all seemed suicidal and had little chance of succeeding. So much he had seen had been false. This could all be a combination of too many holograms. After all, in this surreal time, who could say what was real and what was electronic propaganda. Malcolm knew of Sam's guilt over his mother's death so maybe that vision was all a lie. He was a little ashamed that he had fallen for it. No rational person would try something as foolish as this.

Sam almost turned and walked away.

Suddenly, his mouth was flooded with the bitter taste of acorn mush. He looked at the scar on his hand where the chip had been and saw the obsidian knife in his belt. "Ahwahnee" He whispered, and it renewed his strength. He sighed hard and gathered his strength as he studied the smooth building surfaces. Climbing up was the only way in that would not get him Lasered by sensor Bots or zapped by einsatz gruppe ZZ Goons. On the plus side, the drones were blinded by the fog, as were most of the security cameras.

The Black Dog stirred, and he decided to climb. He was relieved to see that the window washing stations appeared to be deep enough to hold his stanchions and pulleys. Carefully and firmly, he drove in the first metal stanchion and pulled himself five feet above street level. The stanchion jerked slightly but held. Methodically, he made his way up the side until he was at the 26th story. He felt comfortable with his pace. If he could keep up this pace, he would be too high to stop when they discovered him.

From an alleyway across the street, Amon, now dressed in his Hauptsturmführer uniform, watched Sam's climb through Omni Vision glasses and smiled in reluctant admiration. He never dreamed Sam would come and, if so, would never dare such a climb. He pulled on his thick, black leather gloves and turned his collar to the frigid wind. Amon was a denizen of hell and, as such, hated the cold, foggy mornings of the Bay Area. But he figured as soon as this job was done, he would take a trip to Haiti to have fun morphing to a Zombie and scaring the little children. Cautiously, he looked up and down the almost empty street. He crossed the slimy, broken brick-work and moved to the building's service entrance. Once there, he passed through the Retina Scan and entered the building, went into the Service Elevator before he decided to pause and check his gun. With perverted reverence, he withdrew his beloved Walther P38 from his shoulder holster. The preferred sidearm of the day was a Glock 26 Laser with radar aiming, but Amon liked the heft and feel of the Walther P38. He enjoyed the glint off the polished barrel for a moment before checking the load. Satisfied, he replaced the gun and punched the button for the top floor.

Sam felt good about the climb at this point. He was at story number 61, and the technique was working smoothly. The stanchions were holding firm, and his footing was better than he had anticipated. He figured he would make the top floor just in time for the television cameras to film it and get it on the evening news. He believed that even Malcolm's monopoly of broadcast news would have to broadcast such a daring death as Sam planned for him.

Amon exited the elevator and made his way to the roof. He glanced over close to the edge where John still stood before he looked down to see Sam, now only 2 floors below and climbing toward him. Sam was making it too easy of a kill. Amon looked bored as he held his gun at the ready and waited.

Sam was at the 64th-floor level and climbing hard when he noticed the first people gathering below. A strong breeze had cleared most of the fog, and he waved at them. They laughed and lit "fatties" and partied, making Sam pause and wonder if he was on a fool's quest.

Maybe Malcolm was right, and the world be better off without them?

Instead, Sam climbed at a faster rate.

Amon anticipated Sam's imminent arrival. Slowly, he moved even closer to the edge of the roof, looked down, and cackled as he waited. "What fools these humans be!"

Sam moved up to the 66th-floor window and was about to ease up to the roof when a small tremor made the building move, causing Sam to drop several feet before he regained his balance.

Amon's feet wobbled beneath him, and he almost pulled the trigger accidentally. He cursed Saint Andreas, whom he had, once tried to possess, then resumed his firing position.

Sam had been through many earthquakes but never one 66 stories high on the side of a swaying building. He was, temporarily, unnerved as he waited to see if there would be any more tremors. He looked up at his stanchion and was satisfied it was still stable. He took a deep breath, exhaled, then resumed his climb.

Amon despised earthquakes. They were acts of God, and neither he nor Malcolm had any control of them. The slightest tremor made him nervous, but he would not let his gun handshake as he waited in the shadows. He watched as Sam tapped a stanchion in a crevasse to pull up on the roof. He waited until Sam's head peeked over the side and looked up. "Malcolm sends you his regards," Amon said as he aimed at the stanchion, holding Sam's rope, and fired.

Sam braced himself as the bullet bounced harmlessly off the wall two feet above the stanchion.

Amon grinned as he aimed to fire once more.

Sam swung at him, but Amon was too far away.

Amon fired off three rounds. As he did, the building swayed violently, knocking him off his feet. He never saw the bullets hit.

Sam watched in fear as the bullets hit all about the stanchion, blowing plaster all over. The stanchion buckled, and Sam slipped on the rope as the building swayed. He fell three floors before he could grab the rope and dig into the side of the building hard enough to stop his fall. Amon scrambled to his feet and cursed aloud as he moved back to the edge of the roof. He was almost there when Malcolm walked through a door onto the roof.

"What's going on?" Malcolm snarled.

"It's Sam. He's here."

"I know."

"Why would he leave the protection of Yosemite?"

"Because I wished it."

"We can kill him now."

"Kill him? No wonder you never made it out of the seventh circle."

"I…I don't understand, Master?"

"Do you want me to send you back to the Harpies?"

"No! No, please!"

"Then put that gun away, and let's invite our guest to join us."

Amon nodded, put the gun away and stoo d behind Malcolm. Malcolm looked down at Sam, who was hanging on for dear life. "Please come up, Sam."

Sam did a double take until Malcolm offered him a hand. He shrugged and ignored Malcolm until he slipped and started to fall. He almost welcomed the fall but grabbed Malcolm's outstretched hand and let Malcolm help him up. Once on the rooftop, Sam lay motionless a moment before he struggled to his feet.

"Sam! My goodness! You could have used the front door!" Malcolm chortled.

Sam did not reply as he reached for his backpack.

Amon pulled his gun and put it in Sam's face.

"Bring that hand out slow and bring it out empty!" Amon challenged.

"Put your gun away, Amon. Then check his backpack." Malcolm ordered.

Sam started to protest but shrugged.

Amon nodded, opened it, and pulled out the ancient obsidian. knife. "He comes to kill us with this?" He chuckled as he handed it to Malcolm.

"For me, Sam?" Malcolm asked.

"For Ahwahnee!"

"You don't believe I love it as much as you?"

"Hell, no!"

"Hell? Not quite! I will make it a heaven on earth."

"What about the seven-headed beast?"

"A fantasy of yours?"

"So. How are you going to set off all seven super volcanoes, Malcolm?"

Malcolm had to smile. "Who else have you told of this fantasy?"

"Then it is true! You really mean to do it?"

"You spoke of this to Tiye?"

"Which Tiye would that be?"

"The one you wish to make a Queen."

"You deny your lust for her?"

Sam had no quick answer.

"It's ok, Sam. The lust of the flesh is my gift to all." Malcolm held up the obsidian knife. "I have never been anything, but your friend and you come to kill me with this?"

"Ahwahnee magic and your kryptonite!"

"You mortals with your juvenile magic."

Sam held out his right hand. "Well, it freed me from your control, and I am alive to talk about it."

"Not magic all, Sam. I had the kill factor deleted from your implant just in case you did something as foolish as removing it."

"Is that a fact?"

"Yes, Sam. Yours was a tracking chip. I never took control of your free will."

Sam felt chilled to his bones. There was the sting of truth in Malcolm's words. "No! I did not do all I did, of my free will!"

"Why do you continue to lie to yourself? You did it for money and what money brought you."

"Yes, I have done evil, but I am not in your league."

"Yes, you are! You were on board making it easy to take over Yosemite. You knew no one would object to an Ahwahnechee selling out his own people?"

"Ok! Ok! So, let's make amends. You kill yourself with the obsidian knife and I will let Amon do the same to me."

Malcolm shrugged, gripped the obsidian knife, and drove it deep into his chest. It had no effect. He grinned at Sam as he handed him the knife. "Your turn."

Sam gripped the knife and started to stab himself.

"No! Stop him!" Malcolm ordered Amon.

Amon knocked the knife from Sam's hand.

"I applaud your honesty, Sam, but it is not our time." Malcolm said.

"You have a fixation on time. Checked your clock lately?" Sam needled.

Malcolm flinched slightly before he smiled. "I have something else of yours you might like to have." Malcolm said as he withdrew the necklace with the Golden Acorn from his pocket and offered it to Sam.

"Where did you…"

"I thought it was too nice to be tossed away."

"You keep it. I don't need a trinket to do what needs to be done."

"Oh? A man of courage and conviction. I like it, Sam but take it anyway. As a token of our friendship."

Sam thought it over but took the necklace. Looked it over then tossed it back to Malcolm. "I expect that is more of a tracking device than a trinket."

Malcolm chuckled in agreement and let it fall on the floor. "Good, Sam. A timely reality check."

"Don't call me a friend. You know why I came."

"You think of me as evil, Sam?"

"If you aren't Satan, you know him well."

"And this Satan is the source of all the world's troubles. Right?"

"I'm not a big fan of the world. Only Ahwahnee."

"Then blame God for the loss of Ahwahnee!"

"God? I am surprised you can say the name without bursting into flame."

"Before you judge me, just think about one thing."

"Okay. What?"

"I did not throw you out of Eden – *He* did."

"Ahwahnee? Eden? Like the biblical garden?"

"No! A little East of that."

"Oh?"

"It was my throne before the Sons of God were a glimmer of creation."

"I don't understand all that. All I want is for you to stop despoiling it now."

"Did you not enjoy the life I gave you, Sam?"

"Yes! I don't deny that. We did great evil so let's pay the price for it now!"

"How so?"

"Sam moved to the edge of the roof and looked down. "Let's hold hands and go for a walk."

"Sam, if I die all those thousands in my sanctuary will die as well. You want that on your conscious?"

"You took all but a few remnants of my conscious. Let's both take a leap of faith that it will be better for all if we both are dead." Sam held out his hand.

"You were to be of great help to me, Sam. I enjoyed your company and had a place for you in my kingdom to come. Please feel free to ease your conscious by jumping."

"Free? How can anyone be free with all those BVR Holograms you sent to mess with my head."

"Did I force you to watch? Is your faith so weak you could not resist temptation?"

"You implanted your damn chip and destroyed my free will."

"No. You were given a placebo chip. I needed you to come of your own free will."

Sam shook his head in disbelief. It pained him to the depths of his soul that Malcolm was telling the truth.

"You came to me like a starving young man, eating acorn mush, and I gave you the world of fine food and all the comforts of wealth. I must say, no one seemed to enjoy it more than you."

"Yes. A penthouse is better than a teepee. Steak is better than acorn mush. A comfortable mattress is nicer than a fleece blanket on the ground." Sam paused and smiled. "But running free with your bare feet – feeling the good earth of Tuolumne Meadows, looking up to see the majesty of Totockahnoola in the morning mist and cleansing the body in the blessed water of Pywiack Falls is much better for the soul."

"Ah, yes. Your soul."

"You will never have it."

"You offered it without my asking, Sam. I must say your lust for the pleasures of flesh made it easy to take." Malcolm paused and looked a little sad. "But I never did."

Sam looked doubtful, then grinned. "Can I trade it for Ahwahnee?"

"No, Sam."

"Why, with all the world at your feet, must you harm it?"

"I am returning it to the paradise it was before it was infested. by man!"

"No! You are destroying it!"

"It must be cleansed; then it will be restored to its pristine greatness."

"No! You haves no right to…"

"Stop it you hypocrite! You drew up most of the plans before you decided to bestow Sainthood on yourself."

The onerous weight of guilt almost brought Sam to his knees before he gathered the strength to reply. "Okay! Okay. You can take me to hell for my sins, but first you can have the whole damn world. Can't you make your New Eden somewhere else?"

"Afraid not."

"It also belonged to my people!"

Scotty grabbed the hand holding the dagger and almost succeeded in dislodging the blade from Saggara's hand. "God! God! Good God, help me!"

"You call on the false god for help?" Saggara brought the dagger down towards Scotty's heart.

"Not so!" Scotty gritted his teeth. "I call on Akhenaten who knew there was but one God!"

"No! Amon Ra cannot replace the old Gods!" Saggara paused and looked at Scotty with contempt, which quickly turned to a look of terror. He dropped the dagger as a ray of dazzling sunlight poured through a window and blinded him. "Ra! I was going to send him to you...no...no! Aten, I'm sorry!...I...No!" Saggara let out a primeval cry of blood lust, then stopped. He touched his throat and found he was suddenly mute. He choked as he saw his flesh turn furry and his hands grow smaller. He looked at Scotty with more pain than anger in his eyes.

Scotty got to his feet and started to pick up the dagger.

Before he could, it disappeared, and the room was filled with a smell of burned offerings. In the distance they heard a loud rumble.

Scotty and Saggara's eyes met and, for a moment, shared a sense of wonder – then fear.

"Heka! I call on you to bring back the old ways." Saggara went to his knees.

Scotty had only a moment to scoff before they were drowned in a deluge of Nile water.

* * *

In a pristine section of the Florid a Everglades, Beau Jennings steered the airboat hard and fast across the grassy wetland. He had just had good news from his roughnecks. They had hit the gas at twenty-five thousand feet and expected to tap into a gusher any minute. Beau was happy because, if true, this would give him the money to repay his financial backers, particularly Malcolm Mabius. Malcolm had spent millions in hard currency to buy the support of key legislators. Legislators who had pushed through a special exemption to allow drilling here in the pristine reaches of Big Cypress.

Beau pushed the airboat through the thick, wet grass and into deep black water encircled by huge cypress trees dripping with Spanish moss. Nearby, white, and blue Herons speared their breakfast of Grouper while a Snowy Egret looked on, hungrily. Alligators of all sizes stalked the feeding birds while one of the last remaining Florida Panthers watched Beau coming his way. The Panther growled, then turned and fled into the swamp. On the tops of fallen mangrove trees, soft- and hard-shell turtles basked in the warm sun. They were surrounded by the most varied garden of orchids, lilies, and other wildflowers in any sub-tropical wilderness left on earth.

Young deer played a strange game of tag among giant ferns on the many saw grass islet hammocks. They stopped their game to see the last remaining Manatee float to the surface of the water with crude oil foaming out of his silent mouth.

As Beau slowed the airboat to a stop, Slim Jennings, his brother, and job foreman, met him with a wide grin on his face. He jumped in the passenger seat and slapped Beau on the leg.

"Hot dog! You're just in time to see it. Ooohhhh, Lordy! Is it gonna' gosh! We heard a rumble a while ago that sounded like a doomsday trumpet."

"That good, eh?"

"You betcha'! The grade of that gas coming up means the oil is top quality. High-grade crude, dude!"

Beau looked over at the five roughnecks standing around a rapidly spinning drill, spewing crude oil into the pristine water. Seconds later, the earth rumbled. The rumble was deep and unlike any he had ever heard before. It was followed by a series of scary groans and following echoes.

"Jesus! What the hell was that?" Beau wondered.

"Not to worry. Just a shifting of pressure. It's on its way up!"

Slim watched the wellhead intently. "Come on, you beautiful baby. Spit!"

They both fell silent as the drill screeched to a halt so fast it began to crack and the earth started shaking violently beneath the airboat. With a deafening shotgun blast, the drill blew apart, sending bullet-sized pieces of hot metal in all directions followed by a gusher of super-heated, blood-red oil.

"Did we hit a muddy water level?" Beau wondered as he watched the spewing gusher. The blood-red oil-soaked his shirt as the airboat began to sink into a scarlet sea. He wiped his hand on his shirt and looked at the bloody stain. As he watched the droplets of blood, he shivered with fear. "It's blood, Slim. It can't be…it just can't be, but it is real blood!"

Slim stared at the crimson flood that surrounded them. He looked at his brother and bowed his head in reverence as they sank deep into its' depths. "Dear God, almighty! Forgive us. We have finally done it. We done killed the good earth, Beau. We done killed the earth!" he said weakly.

They disappeared into a sea of the Earth's blood before Beau could reply.

CHAPTER FOUR

"**W**here is it?" Malcolm grumped as he sat at his desk. "I couldn't find it, Master!" Amon replied.

"You mean his body just disappeared?"

"No one saw it, Master! I swear no blood on the streets and no eyewitnesses, no…"

"So, he just flew away?"

"Not unless he is an angel!" Amon chuckled.

Malcolm growled and with a wave of his hand sent Amon crashing hard against a wall. "Never suggest that again or you will be given to the Harpies who eat the flesh but leave the nerves exposed to hellfire."

Amon whimpered as he slid down the wall.

"He can't be alive, Master. We think John's followers have hidden the body." Oskar spoke up.

"Not John or his followers. It's an old enemy who is risking much to interfere." Malcolm paused to look dead serious. "Sam must not be allowed to return to Yosemite! Find him. Kill him.

Bring me the body and lay it at my feet!"

"We'll find him, Master!" Oskar and Amon nodded in unison.

"Go now!"

Oskar and Amon started to leave.

"Wait a minute. What's the latest intel on the Carrizo Plain project?" Malcolm demanded.

"Some aseismic activity, but too minor for NEIC monitors to pick up," Oskar replied.

"Yellowstone?"

"Old Faithful is now called Old Unfaithful. It erupts sporadically, and Steamboat is ready to blow!"

Malcolm looked dead serious as he paced the floor then stopped in front of his doomsday clock. It read: 11:59:39. He grimaced, then moved to a window that looked out across the Bay. The sky was blood-red, and huge white caps appeared where no wind was visible. "The winds of woe are picking up. We must hurry!"

Oskar and Amon started to leave again.

"Hold it!" Malcolm called them back.

Oskar and Amon froze.

Malcolm smirked and shook his head in disdain. "Oskar, What's the latest on Sam's relationship with Tiye Adams?"

"He pulled that mad dog routine once too many, and she left him."

"We can count on human love being irrational." Malcolm smiled a tight smile. "What is her last recorded location?"

"We think she is in her apartment." Amon said.

"You think?"

"She has a firewall we haven't been able to penetrate," Oscar spoke up.

"But John Pattos was seen entering their two hours ago," Amon added.

"Seen? Send a Chip ding and confirm it." Malcolm growled.

Amon and Oskar looked at each other, each more afraid to answer than the other before they spoke together. "He...doesn't...

have...before we had a chance, he was..."

"He is not implanted and has escaped?" Malcolm could barely control his anger."

Oskar and Amon gave a weak nod.

"Oh? So, tell me how that happened and how he got out of the top of an Ultra-Secure cell in Isolation?"

"We don't know!" Amon and Oskar fretted and cowered in fear. "What do you mean you don't know?"

Amon looked to Oskar to answer. Oskar backed away and left Amon to reply. Amon glared at Oskar before he turned and answered Malcolm. "We went to get him for a Chip implant...and..."

"And what? Damn it! Tell me now!"

Amon stepped back and glared at Oskar. "Tell him! You were first on the scene!"

Oskar hesitated until Malcolm's glare made him speak. "The Robo Guards were gone, the security monitors were down, his cell door was wide open, and...and he was gone...and...we don't know how...but...."

"But what?" Malcolm almost turned to the Red Dragon.

"There was a pride of Lions in his cell."

Malcolm barely held back his fury as he thought aloud. "Michael and Daniel!"

Amon and Oskar looked puzzled.

Something that happened a long time ago." Malcolm sagged a little before regaining his strength. "The entirety of the Heaven hosts is upon me, but I will still prevail!"

Amon and Oskar nodded cowered agreement.

"Is there no trace of John from the drones?"

"Yes, Master. One spotted him and fired a shot!" Amon brightened.

"Yes, Master, he was headed to Tiye's apartment. The drone wounded him but then malfunctioned." Oskar stepped up.

Malcolm paced the floor angrily, then stopped and scowled. "I will take care of John Pattos and Ms. Abrams! You two find Sam alive or bring me his body!"

Oskar and Amon bowed their way out of the room. Malcolm looked out of his window across the hills toward San Francisco Bay and the city below. He was worried as he saw the deadly Black-Orange sea building up a half-mile off the coast heading inland at this very moment. As he watched it, he heard whispers in the air.

"For he is the living God, and he endures forever. His kingdom will not be destroyed; His dominion will never end. He rescues, and He saves. He performs signs and wonders in the heavens and on the earth. He has rescued Daniel from the power of the lions."

"Shut up, Michael, leave me alone and stay out of this!" He thought it over. "Or continue and join me in ruling. You will find it much more satisfying than serving!" Satan paused to smirk. "Oh, I forgot. You don't have the guts to do that.

Daniel had to grab Michael's arms and hold him back.

CHAPTER FIVE

Each year, to honor his son's birthday, God gave the Angels a stone jar of his son's best wine. It was a much-anticipated celebration because it was a velvet vintage. Many were the frustrations of the Angels, particularly the Guardian Angels, who dealt directly with human foibles, so they needed this one day to themselves.

Michael and the Arch Angels even let down a little and joined in the revelry. They were deep into their cups when the first signs of rebellion surfaced. Michael knew of their frustration at the delay in Judgment Day and how anxious they were for it to come. What scared him the most was that it was the same mood of rebellion that had caused Lucifer to fall and had loosened evil on the world. He felt it stronger than most and had to fight the urge to pull the Sword of The Word and start the Apocalypse. That urge was so strong he refused to drink any of the wine he loved so much, fearing it might lead him to foolish action.

*   *   *

Sam had fallen 66 stories and was 6 feet from certain death. His only worry was that his body would br e a k , and yet he would live. To ensure that would not happen, he forced himself to keep his head pointed down. Even the fickle gods, who might want to Prolong his agonizing life, could not stop death from coming to a headless man. He wanted the concrete sidewalk to smash through his head-bone, obliterate his brain and every ounce of consciousness that caused him such agony. There was no hope in his soul for another life of any kind. He welcomed oblivion.

In the last instant, inches from death, with a last act of whimsy, he formed his body into a swan dive. He had struggled to keep his eyes open, thinking it would be cowardly to close them. But as the sidewalk was inches from his face, he found his bravado gone and closed them as something deep in his being begged for life. He expected a moment of pain, then an eternity of peace as he whispered a prayer he had heard once. "Now I lay me down to sleep; I pray the Lord my soul…"

Sam did not finish the prayer before he found himself lifted by an unseen hand. Fog hid the hand until Sam found himself looking up at a rider on a Pale Horse. The rider was dressed in a Roman Centurion's uniform but held an Ahwahnechee bow and quiver of arrows. His was not the face of Tenaya but putrid death. In seconds, he took Sam to the top of El Capitan, where Sam looked down on the Ahwahnee Valley. There he saw countless multitudes of people running toward him. For a moment, he did not see what caused them to run. Then he saw a huge Dragon with seven heads begin to devour them. Behind the dragon were legions of Roman soldiers slaying people with their swords. Following them were people fleeing swarms of locusts and dying with open sores on their faces and little children, skeletal from famine, reaching out for a morsel of food.

The few who escaped the Dragon were torn apart by wild beasts. Then he saw the hedonist depravity of congregations of Godless people performing every vile act of evil debauchery. There are scenes of empty churches and people kneeling before graven images.

The Horseman looked upon them with scorn. "Although they may fast, I will not listen to their cry! Although they may offer burnt offerings and grain offerings, I will not accept them. Instead, I will f… h them off by sword and famine and plague." The Horseman …dered and vanished.

Moments later, Sam saw a vision of a hand holding a scroll that was sealed with seven seals. Four of the seals were broken. He reached for the scroll but was carried on a warm wind that made him feel young and happy. He was a schoolboy with no worries and with the playful notions of a child. He delighted in carefree feeling and wondered if he was wrong and there might be a heaven. He saw only fog, and when it cleared, he found himself standing on the sidewalk listening to the sound of Christmas music.

Sam had not heard carols sung on the streets of San Francisco in years, and he was not in the mood to listen to them. They were being sung by a handful of John's flock, who were soon silenced by Facistas and einsatz gruppe ZZ Goons using machetes instead of Lasers because they enjoyed the terror machetes caused before the victim was chopped to pieces.

As the carolers fell before the machete chops, their red blood blended with the dark green of a gutter full of discarded Christmas trees.

Sam was too numb to care.

The terrible bouts with his private demons had drained much of his psychic energy, and the greetings of the season rang hollow. He knew he was going mad and was desperate to kill himself.

Yet, how to do it?

He had ridden with death and still walked free. He knew he was no Enoch. His relationship with God was the total opposite of the loving one Enoch had with God. It occurred to him maybe there was a God, and he was being punished for his disbelief. In his fevered mind – he found that amusing.

Sam shuddered with a strange chill and felt overwhelmed by loneliness. It was the first Christmas without Tiye or any friends. Since he considered it a pagan holiday, Christmas was always a downer for Sam. Tiye had been a savior during this time, but this time, he knew he would have to make it alone.

The slaughter of the carolers cast an ominous silence over the streets, and he felt his spirit was about to die. He closed his eyes and rubbed his forehead. He sighed and felt some happiness knowing Tiye was free of him and his special kind of madness. Sam knew many who heard voices and saw strange visions had become psychopathic killers. They all had a Black Dog straining at a leash, He also knew his Black Dog was sleeping now but would not sleep forever, and he might not be able to hold him down next time he saw her.

Sam hoped wherever she was; she was safe and happy.

He began walking aimlessly and, without realizing it, found himself at her apartment building, standing outside her door. He stopped and thought it over, remembering she said the Facistas had burned it down. Or maybe his confused mind was remembering it wrong. He smiled as he recalled the last Christmas they had spent together camping out in Yosemite. They had awakened to a soft snowfall that was almost warm to the touch. As they moved out of their tent, they encountered three young deer sniffing at their backpacks. Tiye delighted in feeding the deer most of their rations. Sam had joined in, and soon, they had a small herd of young deer at their fingertips. Ground squirrels, a coyote, a small Black Bear, and an occasional possum dropped by. It was a heady moment of spiritual communion between humans and animals the Magi would have envied.

Sam had never seen Tiye so happy, and it was the last time he had been free of the torment that, now, ate at his soul. Torment based on the harsh truth that he was partially responsible for the bulldozers cutting down the magnificent Sequoias and crushing Ahwahnee granite to raise insults of steel and glass.

If there was indeed a throne of heaven on earth – it was there. The thought of Malcolm raising an evil throne there made Sam nauseous.

Yet, he knew of no way to stop it now.

Sam stood in front of Tiye's apartment door and started to punch in her code. He pulled back and shrugged with indecision. He wanted to say a last goodbye, yet he did not want to endanger her. He stood in front of the door for a long time, staring at the security camera. If she was watching, he would let her decide to let him in. He sighed hard and was about to turn and leave when the door opened, and Tiye looked at him with a jaundiced eye. She started to close the door, then opened it wide and motioned him in as she moved by her fireplace and sipped a glass of wine. "Who are you?"

Sam entered and shut the door behind him.

"Sam!"

"Sam Rathe is dead."

"A fact or a wish?"'

"It was on the news."

"Since when do you believe Malcolm Media?"

"Only part of it."

"Which part?"

"The part where you tried to kill Malcolm but killed yourself!"

"I feel pretty good for being dead."

"You found a rope to stop the fall?"

"Not exactly."

"There is security footage of you going over the top of his building?"

"I tried to take him down with me."

"I see." Tiye noticed the necklace around his neck. "Your amulet works outside of Yosemite?"

"Maybe. Thanks for leaving it."

"I was hoping you would not find it."

"I know. I had to come."

"You are lucky to be alive."

"I know."

"Whatever happened, it wasn't because of a charm necklace, Sam."

"You are sure? I fell 66 floors and survived?"

Tiye touched the Golden Acorn and shrugged. "Well, something broke your fall. And I would not advise making a habit of jumping off buildings."

Sam chuckled.

They shared a moment of fond remembrance.

Sam looked at the painting of Yosemite with the big black "X" across it. "What a novel painting. A new art form?"

"Yes. You like it?"

"A little less black ink, maybe."

"You can't be here." Tiye turned cold.

"I had to see you."

"You know, he knows you are here, and his Goons are on their way. Malcolm has it on worldwide media. He has posted you as a serial killer, and The Facistas and einsatz Goons are to shoot you on sight."

"Then I am endangering you?"

"Yes....I should be used to it, but don't think so."

Sam turned to leave.

"Hold on!" Tiye called after him. "I need to know. You scared the hell out of me! The truth. How on earth did you break that fall?"

"A horseman." Sam stopped and looked cynical. "You know, like in those new Mega AI BVR holograms you were developing."

"Which holograms?"

"It's ok. Malcolm told me about them...."

"Told you what?"

"It doesn't matter. Your new ones are amazing. Your Horseman saved me. Thanks."

Tiye could barely conceal her anger. "I don't know what Malcolm told you, but he took all my projectors away months ago."

Sam studied her face and eyes, looking for a hint of deception. It radiated righteous indignation instead. "Oh? Then...no, Tiye. I'm sorry. He must have sent one."

"Not likely."

"Yeah!" Sam chuckled. "You believe in angels?"

"Would you like some wine?" Tiye ignored the question.

"I'd better not." Sam smiled at her. "I just came to say goodbye."

"Goodbye."

Sam held the Golden Acorn in his hand. "Thank you."

"I was hoping you wouldn't even look for it."

"Maybe it works here, after all."

"I would put my money on the Holographic horsemen."

"But you didn't send them – right?"

"No, Sam. For the last time I don't have that capability anymore!"

"Why would Malcolm send them?"

"Trying to outguess him will make you crazy."

Sam uttered a cynical chuckle. "I'm way past that already."

Tiye's reply was a sad look of understanding.

41

Sam smiled at her and ached to take her in his arms. Her eyes did not seem receptive. "I am not sure I was even there. I have such weird dreams lately."

"Oh, you were there alright! It's all over Malcolm's. worldwide media."

"Then, I did…"

"The security cameras lost you in the fog, but Malcolm used CGI to show you landing on a ledge, then being rescued by John's followers. It also showed you leading them into Malcolm's office and trying to kill him. He made make you look like a mad dog-killer and had a permission to kill order posted."

"Mad dog?"

"You do have that side, and he has it on tape."

"Has he bothered you?"

"Not yet!"

"Oh? I'm so sorry to have come, Tiye. The last thing in the world I wanted to do, was hurt you in any way."

Tiye sipped her wine and looked at the torment in Sam's face. He looked so gaunt and troubled she could not hold back all her sympathy for his plight or guilt for not helping him. "I wish I knew how to help you."

"You tried. I wish it had worked."

"Me too."

"So, are you stopping speeding locomotives next?" Tiye tried for a laugh.

Sam sighed hard. "If you leaped off a tall building – I would catch you in my arms."

Tiye put down the wine and moved a little closer. "Oh, Sam! I love you, but you have a dangerous side, and we can't fight all he has arrayed against us!"

"He means to destroy the earth."

"There is not much left he hasn't destroyed."

"There is Ahwahnee."

"Say that again."

"Ahwahnee?"

"When did you find you could say that?"

Sam had to think it over. "When you sent the hologram…when I saw…I don't know. Maybe the waters of Pywiack cleansed me."

"Why did you leave it? You had sanctuary there."

"You know the answer. I had to try to get in that control room and destroy his servo mechanisms."

"A fool's errand. They aren't there anymore."

Sam looked sad, then smiled. "So, someone must prowl around his Temple attic?"

"Don't look at me. I'm in survival mode."

Sam nodded understanding. "You aren't safe here, Tiye. If he finds a way to blow the seven super volcanoes, it will all be over. Don't you understand that!"

"Yes, Sam. You go…go to Yose…Ahwahnee and find a way to stop him!"

"Me? Sorry, that is a job for Super Duper Computer girl!" Sam looked at her with love. "Please come with me. I will help you. I have seen the inside of his temple."

Tiye grimaced and looked embarrassed.

Sam was visibly stunned. "You! You have been there also?" Tiye shrugged.

Sam sniffed betrayal. The Black Dog began to awake.

Tiye backed away gave Sam a serious look. "I thought you could control your canine friend." Tiye picked up her BVR Phone and punched in a number. A hologram of a PRG (Private Robo Guard), appeared.

"You wish to report?" The PRG intoned.

"Standby mode, please." Tiye lay the phone down but kept her finger close to it. She looked at Sam with affection. "Yosemite is my favorite place in the whole world, and If I thought, for a minute, anything we could do would stop laser blasts and bulldozers, I would be there at your side."

"You will die here. Tiye!"

"Maybe there are some things I can do to avoid that."

The Black Dog awoke and snarled. "What kind of deal have you made with him?"

"Do you believe I love you, Sam?" Tiye put her finger on the PRG call button and looked for any sign of The Black Dog fully awakened.

Sam trembled with indecision. He forced the Black Dog to sit. "I don't know what to believe anymore.' He looked at her with love. "But I will go because I will not allow my dark soul to ever harm you."

"Sam! Please be careful. There is an APB out on you…."

"If I am to die, it will be in a place my soul loves."

"I love The City, Sam."

"The City won't be here in a few days!" Sam looked at the disbelief in Tiye's eyes and sighed with frustration. "As the song goes, you don't have to be a weatherman to know which way the wind is blowing."

"According to you, straight from hell."

"At terminal velocity!"

"So, Judgement Day is coming?"

"I didn't say that. But it is Judgment Day Eve?"

"The horsemen told you?"

"No! Every day is Judgment Day Eve."

"Yes, Sam. That is true!" John Pattos entered the room.

"John? How…what are you doing here?"

"Tiye was kind enough to take me in." John smiled at Tiye.

Sam looked at John with suspicion. "Malcom let you go free?"

"No, Sam. It was divine intervention."

"Sam shook his head in disdain. "You guys expect me to believe Malcolm would allow two of his worst enemies to be alive and free?

"Did you not escape death by the hand of God, Sam?"

Sam stepped back in disbelief. "No, No! Both of you have made pacts with Satan!"

"Not true. God opened my cell doors and saw me safely from the Lion's Den. Malcolm wants us to worship him. Maybe instead, we will have an old-fashioned revival and flood his evil sanctuary with prayer."

"Wake up you stupid Holy Joe! It's all his plan and you are falling for it." Sam looked at Tiye who was about to summon help. "Ty, you know enough about geology to know a major quake is always

Amon appeared beside Malcolm. "Yes, he helped with the transporting his own people to the ovens. I think he liked the work." Amon smirked.

"No! You are the prince of liars. I don't believe any of it." Tiye snapped.

"You loved him, and you feel his guilt, do you not?" Malcolm posed.

"No!"

"Now, who is the liar."

Tiye watched as Jacob was pelted by an avalanche of bones that buried him up to his neck.

"Rina! Help!" Jacob called out.

Seconds later, Malcolm closed the portal.

Tiye glared at Malcolm. "Even if real, there is nothing I can do about it."

"Wrong. You can do a lot for him. Consider Gehinnom a Laundromat for the soul. I own it while the soul is being washed. I can see to it that the rinse cycle is speeded up, and less bleach is applied." Malcolm glared and surrounded Tiye with a dark aura. Suddenly she felt the pain of a great weight on her shoulders and had to drop to her knees. "You are feeling is a small portion of your Grandfather's guilt. Once your people relieved guilt with animal sacrifice. How will you relieve his?"

"No! Stop! Please!"

Malcolm waved his hand, and the aura and pain vanished.

Tiye got to her feet and grimaced. "You don't get it! Sam doesn't trust me, so he won't give up that necklace."

"The necklace is of little concern to me."

"What?"

"It is but a dime-store trinket with some small powers."

"Then what is all this about?"

"Has he spoken of a Tree or a book?"

"I have no idea what you are talking about."

"I am talking about your lover, boy. If he gets past my security and makes it inside Yosemite, you can and will find out what he has been called to do!" He stopped and looked dead serious. "For your grandfather's sake?"

"He is not going to Yosemite. You saw to that with the lie about his heritage."

"It was no lie."

"Look, you have shut down all my systems and made Sam so crazy he is harmless. What else do you want from me?"

Malcolm looked at her with love. "I want you to be my Queen and obey my every command!"

Tiye did not reply as she watched John, on his knees with his head bowed praying hard. He looked up at her and pleaded with his eyes for her to agree.

"In name only. No Donavan episodes?"

"It will begin that way if you wish. But soon you will beg to come to me." Malcolm was pleased with himself.

Tiye was defiant for a moment before she felt compelled to fall to her knees and ow in reverence.

Sam walked slow and sad as the strange crimson San Francisco fog closed around him. Without realizing it, he found himself on the Golden Gate Bridge. He could not see far ahead but heard mumbled prayers, then seconds later, a splash into the bay. He envied the peace they had found. As he walked, he felt a huge sense of loss. Tiye was the only thing worth living for. Maybe she was right. It was foolish to think he could go up against all the forces Malcolm Mabius had gathered. What could be better than dying in her arms? He stopped and thought about going back when the fog cleared, and he looked down to see he was standing on the top of a tower of the Golden Gate Bridge.

Seven hundred feet below, he saw the halfway-to-hell safety net rigged up for bridge workers long ago. It was filled with hundreds of dead and dying people holding out their arms for help. He watched as some died of starvation, others by horrible plagues, and many were torn apart by wild beasts. The waters of the Bay boiled and began to give up the dead. They were reborn but just as quickly struck down with a fiery sword by a rider on a pale green horse. As they were struck down, the waters parted and exposed the fires of Hell.

All descended into it.

Their cries were so loud they hurt Sam's ears. He watched with envy as the fire consumed them. He could feel the heat on his face as he leaped to join them. There was no sensation of falling, and he let out a cynical chuckle expecting to be saved by a Horseman.

He wondered what color it would be this time.

Instead, he found himself wanting to hold Tiye and die in her arms. He found he was not falling but running to where he thought she would be. He did not stop until he found himself back at Tiye's apartment. Once there, he stopped and stared at the door and almost turned to go when he noticed it was partially open. He decided to check it out and slowly opened the door and went in.

He was shocked by what he saw.

Tiye's apartment was empty.

Sam looked around frantically trying to find her but neither she nor John were to be found. He stood in the middle of her living room looking dejected until he was interrupted by a mega BVR Holocast. He wanted to puke when he saw Malcolm's smiling face. He was standing on a Train Platform beneath the sign that read "Oakland Terminal." Immediately behind him on the railroad tracks was a line of ultra-modern rail cars. Inside the cars, Sam could see people nicely dressed and smiling as if they were going on a fun vacation. He scoffed when he saw Tiye and John Pattos greeting and helping people board the train.

"I must say, Malcolm, your new projectors and production standards are superb. Give me compliments to Ty!"

"Thank you, Sam. Why don't you tell her yourself?" Malcolm turned and waved to Tiye and John to join him.

Tiye walked up with an endearing smile on her face.

John John Pattos followed behind her, smiling as well.

"You can turn off the projector, Malcolm. I am not buying it."

"Miss Adams, please tell our cynical friend you are very real." Malcolm grinned.

"I'm okay, Sam. You said yourself that The City is due for a major quake. It is unsafe for anyone to be there."

"So, you believe you are safer with Beelzebub?"

"Oh, Sam. My goodness! What are you some latter-day Philistine?" Malcolm chuckled.

"Perhaps." Sam looked at John. "What about you, John. You know better."

"He has offered to build a Tabernacle for me and my flock, Sam." John smiled.

"How does it feel to be devoid of a soul?" Sam huffed.

"No, Sam. As you can see, he has offered us all safe passage to Yosemite and will allow us to hold our service without interference." John Pattos beamed.

"You believe the great deceiver?"

"It's best for all to believe him, Sam." Tiye stepped in front of John.

"Tiye! My, God Tiye! For God's sake Wake Up!"

Tiye looked sad, and tears formed in her eyes. "Please do not follow, Sam. Our lives and the lives of the thousands on the train depend on it."

"Ah, yes, now comes the rub."

"Everyone's safety depends on you not coming to Yosemite. That is best for all. I have told Building Security to let you have access to my place for as long as you want to stay."

"Really? I don't like cold beds."

"Malcolm guarantees us safety if you stay away." Tiye pleaded.

"I confirm the truth of what she says and that to which we have agreed for safe passage for all. Please, Sam! "Do not come to Yosemite," John added.

"Come on, John. You believe what the most deceitful being in history tells you?"

John's eyes revealed great pain for a moment before he replied. "What happens in Yosemite will decide the fate of all."

"Maybe that's a reason I should come."

Malcolm stepped in front of John. "You are a very selfish person, Sam. You risk everyone's safety for some insane notion that you have the power to stop a project that you were, once, very much a part of."

"Well, I don't think I'll be sticking around here waiting for the sky to fall. Think you could give me a cot and a couple of hots in that Temple of yours for old times' sake, Malcolm?"

"You promise to be a good boy and not bring along any stray pets?" Malcolm chided.

"No promises. Just keep the light on. Who knows. Maybe I'll stop by."

Tiye stepped up with a stern gaze.

It hurt to see Tiye captive and realize she was lost to him. The bile of betrayal was almost as bitter as acorn mush. "Save me some wedding cake, Queen Lil!"

"Sam, you will put everyone's life in danger. If what we had meant anything – please don't come." Tiye reached out and their hands almost touched before the Holocast faded.

After the Holocast faded, Sam saw Tiye's SatPhone on a nearby table. He picked it up and had to fumble with it to get it going. Once he did, a miniHolographic image of Tiye appeared. She looked at him with love and pleading eyes. "Please help me!"

Sam turned it off and ran to catch the train to Ahwahnee.
APOCALYPSE COMETH

CHAPTER SIX

Ahmid Razzon had lived through countless sandstorms in his sixty-five years on the desert, but he had never seen one come up so fast. One minute he was kicked back in his new government-built housing, putting a blanket over his new color television; the sand was blowing in through his windows. Ahmid had left the windows open on purpose. He was still angry that the government had forced him to air-condition his house. Ahmid did not trust anything made by the hand of man. Sweat was natural. Air conditioning and televisions were abominations. As the winds increased, he hurried to close his windows. Ahmid listened intently as the storm began a howling that reminded Ahmid of the howl of a wounded animal.

It took all of his strength, but he finally got all the windows closed. He was sad to see they were not closed in time to protect his hand-sewn carpets.

The carpets were covered with an inch of strange-looking garnet and white sand. Curiously, Ahmid reached down and picked up a handful of the sand and examined it. He had never seen sand that sparkled so brightly and so resembled crushed diamonds and red velvet. Slowly, he shook his head in wonder that the desert he knew so well had suddenly changed colors. He moved to the window to look upon this wonder. He was stunned to see that the storm had passed as suddenly as it had come. Shrugging that it was God's will,

Ahmid moved to open his window once again. As he did, he noticed a suspended cloud of brightly colored sand hovering a mile from his house. The strange cloud measured at least ten miles wide and floated five feet off the ground. It seemed to be heading his way.

So bright was the sparkle from the dazzling white and red sand cloud that Ahmid could look at it for only a moment.

Hurriedly, he found his sunglasses then looked upon them directly.

Ahmid's fascination turned to horror as he watched the sand cloud envelope his neighbor's house and began to whirl around it in a murderous sand vortex.

The sand acted like some giant sanding machine gone wild.

Ahmid's first impulse was to run. He was mad at himself for that thought as he moved to his prayer rug and kneeled reverently. Humbly, he prayed that the menace would pass over his house. As he prayed, he heard the rasping noise of the sand cutting away at the outside of his home.

In a few seconds, it was through the stucco walls. It blew Ahmid's television out of a window along with all his other furnishings as he prayed even harder.

All about him was turbulence and cutting sand, but Ahmid's clothes did not rustle.

With one last long roar, the winds passed, leaving him alone in a house – empty but for Ahmid and his prayer rug.

Ahmid looked heavenward and whispered prayers of thanksgiving. The wind had left is home free of all devices made by man. With the air conditioner gone he now felt honest sweat begin to exude from his body. The place where the TV had sat was now a book stand with an open Koran upon it. A covey of Chukar Partridges began to sing outside his window. A sound he had not delighted in for years.

Ahmid was so serenely happy he bent down and, reverently, kissed his prayer rug.

*   *   *

For ten years, fishers off the Northern California and Oregon coast had experienced the dreaded Black-Orange tide. No one knew where it came from or what caused it. They only knew that it began about twenty miles out to sea and moved inland, killing any fish trapped in its fifty miles long, ten-foot-deep mantle.

Fast Eddie, the clandestine factory ship Captain, had hoped it would not come this year. But there had been nothing normal about this year and he was extremely disappointed to hear the Coast Guard announce over his radio that it had been spotted only two miles off his port bow. Fast Eddie knew that would limit his catch of large tuna. But he figured he could always stretch the load by mixing in dolphin meat. He shrugged as he ordered his men to pull in his nets as fast as they could to salvage as much of a catch as possible. His movements were hampered by a sudden wind that blew cold out of the south and caused his boat to rock in what were now very choppy seas.

Fast Eddie shook his head in disgust as he contemplated how hard it was to make a good living as a poaching fisher these days. He looked on angrily at the nets that finally spilled over onto the deck of his old ship. The spilling nets revealed a meager haul of undersized tuna with a good catch of screaming and squirming dolphins. He was so busy loading his gun to shoot the dolphins; he didn't notice the Black-Orange ooze around the starboard border of his ship. The Black-Orange goolapped at the ship and instantly began bleaching the rusted metal hull.

Fast Eddie aimed and fired at the head of one of the smaller dolphins. The bullet bounced, harmlessly, off the deck. He aimed again. The small dolphin seemed to look at him and beg for mercy. Fast Eddie ignored the plea as he squeezed the trigger. The bullet hit just in front of the small dolphin, causing it to squeal as it fought to squirm off the deck.

Fast Eddie cursed his marksmanship as he started to aim again. He ignored the cries of his men, who pointed to the Black-Orange tide now surrounding the ship. It burned through the hull and poured into the ship's engine room, melting everything in its path.

Fast Eddie aimed once more. The small dolphin seemed to crouch in fear as Fast Eddie squeezed the trigger. He was unable to pull the trigger as the Black-Orange slime hit the boiler in the engine room and exploded. The explosion blew the ship apart. Fast Eddie and his men were exploded into a bloody rain of human chum.

The small dolphin and his brethren fell softly to the ocean as the Black-Orange tide quickly receded. They gathered in a circle and chatted a moment happily before they swam off laughing.

* * *

The light blue ozone layer had been thinning out for years. On Christmas morning, it stretched and waned and finally disappeared. High above New York City, a hole fifty miles wide formed a perfect circle that poured unobstructed ultraviolet rays and high-intensity radioactive particles.

Twenty miles below, Janice DeLong, a leggy, blonde high fashion model with a flawless complexion and shiny hazel eyes, clicked along 52nd street on her way to what she hoped would be a very lucrative appointment.

Janice ignored the bad air and failing climate. She was totally focused on herself. She had left two husbands and three kids behind to get to this point in her career and she was not going to let anything stop her now. Hers was a world of mirrors all looking her way.

For the last eight years, Janice had worked at a smattering of poorly paid freelance modeling jobs. She was happy this day because the Williams agency had liked her previous layout and offered her a chance to audition. She had worked on her hair and face for three hours and had lain in the sun for six, getting ready for this appointment.

Janice felt simply beautiful as the cool breeze tossed her long blonde hair playfully. She was smiling as she was only a few yards from William's building. Soon, she would have her chance, and she would make the most of it. She paused just outside the huge glass door as she felt itchiness in her right hand.

She was horrified to look down and find a large red welt in the middle of it.

The lesion seemed to increase in size as she watched it. Suddenly, her face felt itchy, and she started to scratch it. She was in a near panic as she took out her compact and checked herself in the mirror. The face that looked back at her in the mirror was covered with large red welts, and she looked as if she had been stung by a hundred bees.

She was about to scream at her fate when a man staggered up beside her, shrieking in agony. The man looked like a leper with large sores all over his face. He reached out for her with a boil-encrusted hand. As Janice reeled backward in horror, he caught fire right before her eyes. All about her, people began breaking out in scores, and many ran blindly into the paths of oncoming cars.

Janice cried out in agony as she smashed the mirror on the sidewalk, only to see her hideous reflection mirrored a thousand times.

A reflection she would never look upon again.

*　　*　　*

Father Timothy, the Franciscan in charge of the Latin Rite of the Church of The Holy Sepulcher in Jerusalem, was worried. Tensions ran high among the various Christian sects charged with maintaining this holiest shrine. Ever since the Easter procession, the Armenian, Greek, and Catholic prelates have been sniping at each other. The dispute was over whose prayer time and whose limited space had been compromised. Father Alexander Nicaea, the Greek Orthodox Patriarch, and Father Timothy had been close friends. But on Easter Sunday, that had ended.

Though their sects celebrated Easter on different Sundays, the small confines of the church made it difficult to have an orderly procession without stepping on someone's toes. The Latin Rites' Chapel of the Apparition was on the route of the Greek Orthodox procession, and some altar servers had tipped over some candles. In addition, Father Alexander felt the Franciscans had exceeded their prayer time of 4:00 am to 7:00 am by some twenty minutes.

Father Timothy had tried to keep the peace. But Father Gregory, the Armenian Patriarch, insisted it was the Greeks who had violated the strict status quo. The Greeks were equally adamant it was the Franciscan's fault.

Father Timothy often wondered if God cared about these petty squabbles. After all, this was the site where Christ was supposed to have ascended to heaven leaving behind the admonition to "…love one another as I have loved you."

Also, everyone was preparing for the End times in their on way. All religions were certain Judgement Day was coming soon.

As he knelt with his fellow Franciscans to say his Liturgy of the Hours, he prayed God would heal this "family" dispute.

Of late, Father Timothy had felt closer to God, hoping to and he had an inner glow as he began to chant. He was delighted in the sound of his fellow Franciscans joining in. Before long, the Chapel of the Blessed Sacrament was filled with a melodious prayer that gave Father Timothy great comfort, until he heard unusual singing. He turned to see Father Alexander and Father Gregory kneeling beside him, and the chapel filled with the faithful of all sects.

A great light flooded the chamber as they all bowed their heads in humility – and knew the status quo – mattered not.

*　　*　　*

Despite his history of fainting spells and epileptic seizures, Little Jimmy Long was determined to be the first man to make the run across Death Valley non-stop. He had trained for two years, running as much as thirty-five miles a day. He had religiously abstained from alcohol, prepared foods, sex, and sweets. He survived only on recommended fruits, nuts, carbohydrate-loading formulas and treated his fainting problem with Chinese herbs. He had fainted only once in the last few weeks and thought it was under control.

If not, he would still rather die running.

As the desert sun slowly brought weak, gray dawn to the desert floor, Little Jimmy looked out at the endless expanse of hard-packed salt. Then he took three deep breaths and broke into a measured pace.

Fifty miles away in the high Sierras, the rain was falling harder than it had for any three hours in the recorded history of the Dowdville weather bureau.

Almost twelve inches in a little over three hours.

Big Jim Long, the part-time meteorologist, looked out of his window at the eerie rain and shook his head. He had never seen anything like it. He had felt it coming into his bones for weeks and worried about his son, Little Jimmy. Big Jim studied the sooty texture of the raindrops against his windowpane. He cursed anyone who had ever poured any pollutant into the sky. He pulled his hand-knitted sweater tight around his frail bones and hoped all good people were safely on high ground.

He bowed his head and said a silent prayer for anyone at sea level. There would be hell to pay when this run-off reached the desert floor. The desert floor where he knew, against his advice, Little Jimmy was, even now, attempting his run.

Little Jimmy was comfortable with the pace he had set for himself. It felt good running on the relatively soft dirt of the Arroyo. He could tell the canyon had once been a river, and it was a welcome relief to the hard pack of the rest of the desert. He had been running now for four hours and felt optimistic until his hands began to tremble, and he felt a seizure coming on. He used all his willpower to fight off the episode and was relieved to feel it go away.

Then he noticed the first trickle of water come around the bend a half-mile ahead. He hesitated for a split second, then picked up his pace slightly. The trickle quickly turned into a rapid flow that rose three inches deep as it foamed at his feet.

Little Jimmy looked up at the limestone walls of the arroyo in anticipation of going to higher ground. He stopped in abject horror as a rolling ball of rattlesnakes bore down on him. Little Jimmy leaped and crawled up the slippery sides of the canyon as the snake ball rolled past. The chorus of hissing and orchestra of rattles made his skin crawl, but he sighed in relief as they narrowly missed him.

Little Jimmy was almost out of the canyon when a river of scorpions floating on giant cacti with razor-sharp needles bore down on him. He turned to go back into the canyon and was felled by a severe

rush of nausea – and a fainting spell. He fought to stay conscious as the desert fell, suddenly quiet.

He sighed in relief as his seizure passed and started running once again. This time faster than he ever had before. "If only someone had a clock on me," Little Jimmy thought as he blistered the sand with his running. He was delighting in his successful escape when the hundred-foot-tall wall of muddy water came thundering around the corner. The force of the water blew him out of his expensive jogging shoes. He tumbled with the water saturated with snakes and scorpions. He was bitten and stung many times before became impaled on a cactus cross. A cross that floated on top of the terrible water roared down the canyon toward a cliff with a drop of five hundred feet.

"Oh, God! No!" Little Jimmy cried out. He could say no more as his body contorted in a seizure.

Big Jim sensed his son was in trouble. With quiet determination, he moved to Little Jimmy's room. He looked in the closet and found the leg braces Little Jimmy had worn as a child. He looked at the baseball bat Little Jimmy had never used in a real game. He turned to see the picture by Little Jimmy's bed. It was a photograph of his wife, Grace, with Little Jimmy as a young boy. A young boy with a handicap he never let evoke false sentiment. Grace had lost her life, having been run down by a drunken motorist while she was training for a marathon.

Big Jim missed her terribly.

Reverently, he picked up the photograph, moved to the window, and looked at the dark sky. "Grace, if you're up there, he needs your help! He needs your help bad!" Big Jim pleaded before he became angry with himself. "He had given up prayer the day Grace was killed and swore he would never pray to any God who could allow that to happen.

His answer was a distant clap of thunder, then a heavy silence Big Jim gave the picture a kiss, set it down, and with a heavy heart, moved from the room.

Suddenly, there was a knock at the door.

Slowly, Big Jim opened it.

His heart leaped at what he saw.

There before him, not even sweating, was Little Jimmy with a broad smile on his face.

"Pop! I did it! I did it! I ran all the way and did not fall down or faint once!"

Big Jim embraced his son with joy.

"Dad, you won't believe it. You know I can't swim, and this cactus had me held down and then, all of a sudden, a swam to solid ground like I had always done it."

"Oh son. I'm so happy. Thank God you are safe!" Big Jim looked up at the sky which held only a single cloud.

He smiled as if it seemed to be Grace in Angelic form.

She smiled at him before the cloud faded away.

Little Jimmy looked in his eyes. "You saw something?"

"Yes. You feel like getting dressed."

"Yeah! I'm fine. Why?"

"If we hurry, we can make it to the Underground Church service."

"You mean risk being shot by the Facistas?"

"Yes."

Little Jimmy looked reluctant, then grinned. "I'm glad you asked. Mother told me she thought you might."

They laughed together.

Michael nodded approval as he stood by Grace, a newly enthroned guardian angel. Grace fluttered her wings with delight. Gabriel shook his head in dismay.

CHAPTER SEVEN

Michael was amused by the boring notion of Heaven most humans held. The belief that the heavenly hosts sat around all day singing hymns in perfect harmony and that all the loved ones who fought on Earth got along peacefully in a celestial setting was laughable. Since no lies were permitted in Heaven, some old scores had to be settled with true forgiveness. He enjoyed watching these soul-cleansing sessions. There was much angst when that which was hidden was revealed, but in the end, the truth set all souls free. He was enjoying watching Henry, the Eighth try to make peace with his six wives. They all had a go at him before they enjoyed a tearful reunion.

Michael's thoughts were interrupted by the sound of Gabriel's horn. He ran toward the sound to see Gabriel holding it.

"Has it begun?" Michael asked.

"What?" Gabriel sat and polished his trumpet.

"You blew the horn!"

"I was just practicing."

"Don't do that!"

"Do what?"

"Don't do that – until it is for real!"

"You need to settle down, Michael."

"Don't you see the rampant perversion of grace so that evil prevails?"

"It will end."

"When? If not stopped, Lucifer will create a new earth with his throne upon it."

"You are not known for your patience." Gabriel smiled.

"Patience is for messenger angels. I am a warrior!"

"We are worried you have done too much already."

"Did I not do as much for Daniel against the Persian Kings?"

"Please mind your pride and act only on the authority of God."

Michael had his hand on the handle of The Sword of the Word. He took it off, sat down and sighed hard.

*　　*　　*

Satan was hard at work preparing the Earth for his takeover.

The earth breathed fire at fifty-foot intervals all along Market Street. As the tourist crowd gawked, ten-foot holes opened, and people dropped out of sight like ducks in a shooting gallery. In the time it takes for a cable car to ring a bell, a thousand geysers blew steam from the Embarcadero to Twin Peaks.

There was no definable epicenter on earth.

The circum-pacific belt was just another earthquake area. There were major earthquakes where no fault existed and no seismic pattern in evidence. There were orogenic belts all over the earth, erosion without rainfall with soil stability, and shallow seas running with high tides. The geosynclines slept no more, and their awakening was awesome to behold. Physical systems were changing at a rate one thousand times faster than at any time in the history of geologic time. All the static energy bases were rapidly modified into kinetic expressions.

Atmospheric, oceanic circulation was in imbalance and the gravity flow of the earth's water supply did not obey the normal laws. Any question of radiation balance was out of the question. Amazon land masses denuded themselves, and rivers spilled over their banks without reason. Huge rocks walked like men. The historically slow convectional movements of the earth's mantle reached unimagined proportions.

Diastrophism was rampant.

The mantle, the crust, the earth's very skin was coming apart. Parts of the lithosphere shell broke apart like plastic veneer. There was a buildup of a massive escape of mechanical energy of such dynamic proportions that no one could measure its magnitude.

All was blamed on climate change caused by man. Few recognized it as the first days of the tribulation.

All systems worked to spread fear and cause many to turn to Malcolm, the anti-Christ, to save them.

All except John's faithful.

Malcolm still did not understand how they could resist him. He dressed in spotless garments; he smiled a beatific smile and offered them safety for freedom. His magnificent Temple only had room for 144.000 so others who came to him had to accept the new microchip and agree to move to "safe" camps.

The camps were far from safe. Many sent to them vanished without a trace.

All but The Keepers being sent to Yosemite.

Sam was one of the few people left who was not under Malcolm's control. He had to give Malcolm credit for removing the instant death trigger from the chip he had implanted in Sam. He did not ponder that thought long. Instead, his thoughts turned to the torment of love and trust. He wondered if Tiye's call for help was a plan was to lure him to his death, or did she really want his help. He felt he was not worthy of going to Ahwahnee, that all his visions had been phony Holograms – but he would go for her.

But to what end?

Sam knew he had only a few days at the most to stop Malcolm, and he had no idea how to do that or even how to get back to Yosemite. Right now, he was busy trying to survive in a city crumbling around him. He kept to the shadows dodging roving gangs of Facistas and einsatz gruppe ZZ Goons who killed just for fun. He stopped and looked back to see the big Bank of the World building shift two miles behind him, and the top began to crack. Seconds later, the 100-story tall Bank Building imploded, and the sky filled with useless currency. He was barely able to avoid the panic that ensued as people who survived the hot steam ran for any transportation available. All the interstate highways and side roads were full of sinkholes, and the only way to Yosemite was to go by rail to Merced and take Yart transport from there.

The problem was how to get by the security and get a seat when everyone was scrambling to board.

Malcolm had megaBVR Holograms of Sam as a fugitive wanted for murder broadcasting worldwide. The Holograms showed him killing women and children with rapid-fire GatLasers. He saw two Robo Cops and a squad of einsatz gruppe ZZ Goons coming his way and ducked into an alley and leaned against a cool brick wall. He sighed hard as he slid down the wall and sat still. The air was oppressive with thin veils of vapors that smelled of new death and rotting corpses. He grinned a sardonic grin and thought maybe he should help Malcolm cleanse this sewer of a City and the rest of the decadent world.

After all, he had lived a good life in Malcolm's employ and maybe Malcolm was the worthy one meant to save Ahwahnee. It was hard for Sam to admit he was wrong. Malcolm did have the power to restore Ahwahnee if only a virtual one. He felt a sense of relief as he decided he would go to Ahwahnee, not to stop Malcolm but to help him.

It was a sensible thing to do.

After all, if this was the "*Time of Jacob's Trouble*" that had to do with Israel – and was of no concern of his.

Sam gripped the Golden Acorn and started to pull it off his neck. He stopped when he saw a vision of himself beside his mother's hospital bed.

"Who are you?" Totuya looked shocked.

"It's me, Mother. Your son."

She looked over his Jeri curl, surgically reduced cheekbones and implant-enhanced blue eyes then shook her head. "No! You are not my son!"

"Mother, they intend to kill me and destroy Yosemite!"

"Yosemite? A Miwok slur! Why do you use it?"

"Am I Ahwahnechee?"

"Why do you ask this?"

"I heard the Paiute Elders tell you we were of Savage blood."

"What does your spirit tell you?"

"When I bathe in the waters of Pywiack I feel I am home."

"Do you love Ahwahnee with all your heart and soul?"

"No one loves it more than I."

"Then go and help to restore it to the Eden it once was!"

"You wish me to help the evil one?"

"You will find you calling there."

His mother's eyes filled with tears as she faded. As his mother's image faded, Sam smelled deceit. "Please, Malcolm. No more holograms. Just leave me alone and do what you will with Yosemite.'"

Moments later, Tenaya, sitting on his Cayuse pony in full war dress, appeared and looked at Sam with eyes fierce with anger. "You would turn your back on your people once again!"

"You can send all the holograms you want. I am not listening anymore!"

"If you allow the evil one to destroy Ahwahnee you will be as the Yellow Dog and cast out forever."

"Don't call me, yellow!"

"Why not? You cower here in the darkness while Ahwahnee is defiled by the evil one."

"I told you. I am not listening. Besides. only a fool would go up against his legions alone."

"Tenaya was joined by a host of Ahwahnechee Angels on horseback in full war dress. "You have never been alone. Did you not fall into the arms of Ahwahnechee Angels?"

Sam looked upon them and felt a sense of belonging. If it was a hologram, he wished to become part of it. He shuddered as he remembered falling and being stopped inches from death. He looked upon Tenaya and the other Ahwahnechee angels and his loneliness eased.

Sam was about to reply when the wall behind him disintegrated under the force of Laser Blasts. He looked up to see a dozen einstaz ZZ goons headed his way, firing as they approached. The shrapnel that peppered his face told him he was not in a vision and this was no hologram. The ZZ goons had Sam cornered and were about to fire again when a volley of Obsidian tipped arrows tore into them killing them all instantly.

"Please let me ride with you."

"You ride with us only when you have earned it." The riders faded away.

Sam wanted to dismiss it as another Malcolm Holocast, but the bodies of the dead ZZ goons lay before him. He sighed hard, picked up and looked into a broken mirror. As Sam gazed into the mirror, he saw himself as a young boy dressed in buckskin playing Ahwahnechee warrior in Tuolumne Meadows. His cheekbones were bigger, his hair was darker and straighter, and his false blue eyes had turned back to the golden hue of a fawn. A small herd of young deer came to play with him and even a Black Bear and a host of forest animals romped at his side. He tripped on a fallen acorn and almost fell. He looked at the acorn, picked it up and almost threw it away. Instead, he found a piece of sharp obsidian, dug a hole, and planted it. He stood up and watched as it grew into a Black Oak laden with thousands of acorns which fell to the ground. The herd of young deer, the Black Bear and all the forest animals came to feed on the acorns. Just as they began to enjoy eating the acorns, the tree and acorns vanished. and all the animals withered and died of hunger. He looked around at garish buildings filling the valley, growing so tall they blocked out the sun. What he saw hurt his soul so much he ran until he found himself at the Pywiack Cascade. He ran to the water to rid himself of the vision. He was almost there when the water turned to dust.

The Black Dog stirred, and Sam awoke screaming.

Though the dream had ended, he knew who he was and what he must do.

Sam had been sleeping in an alley across from Tiye's apartment building, and once he rubbed the sleep out of his eyes, he stepped back in horror. There was a vacant lot where Tiye's apartment building once stood. Smoke wafted off a pile of stone debris.

Malcolm had vaporized her building and most of the others nearby.

Sam was relieved to know she was alive. He had only traces of regret that she would be Malcolm's bride. He was not going to Ahwahnee to save her. He had to save the holy waters of Pywiack and in so doing save himself. He moved down the sidewalk and stopped at a huge megaBVR monitor mounted on top of every building still standing, broadcasting one of Malcolm's sermons live from Cathedral Towers. He wondered how long he had been sleeping as he hailed the nearest Robo Taxi.

The Robo Taxi tried to ignore him, but Sam stepped in front of it knowing its sensors would make it stop for a pedestrian.

It stopped only inches from his body.

The Robo Taxi Dispatcher on the dashboard BVR video Monitor fumed with electronic rage. "You will be reported to Transit Central!"

Sam jumped in the taxi. "Shut up and get me to the Oakland Train Terminal. And hurry!" Sam chortled into the monitor.

The Dispatcher smirked. "Insert Bitcoin or Transit Card into the lighted slot."

"I don't have either of those?"

"Please exit the vehicle – immediately!"

"Look! Just go! Now!" Sam demanded as his door swung open and an alarm sounded. He thought it over as he listened to the alarm and watched the condescending look on the Dispatcher's face. He knew the Robo Taxi had an emergency override for manual control, so he leaped into the front seat and looked for the control switch.

"Return to your seat, Sir!"

Sam ignored him and searched for the control switch.

"You have 30 seconds to return to the passenger area, or einsatz gruppe Byar will be forced to remove you!"

"Go to hell!" I must get to the Oakland Terminal. It's a matter of life and death."

"Insufficient cause for your actions. This vehicle will be locked down, and you will be apprehended and detained." The Dispatcher said as the engine died.

The loud alarm was ringing in Sam's ears as he finally found the manual control switch under the dash, He flicked it on, and his heart sank as the alarm did not stop and the engine did not turn back on.

"Oh, Tenaya! Please!" Sam pleaded as he held the Golden Acorn tight in his hand.

The alarm seemed to get louder, and he could see Three einsatz gruppe ZZ Goons with Laser guns and a dozen Facistas wielding machetes heading his way. He gripped the Golden Acorn even tighter and was wondering which way to run as einsatz gruppe ZZ Goons aimed their guns at him and fired near misses.

They were almost at the Robo Taxi when the engine started. Sam leaped into the driver's seat, gunned the engine, and drove hard.

The ZZ Goons and Facistas scattered as he roared by them. Sam dodged in and out of the fallen debris to protect himself from their fire which exploded all around him. Soon he was out of range but did not slow down until he ran into general chaos and people running for their lives. He knew the main streets would be too choked with people, so he took back alleys and side streets until he found a ramp onto the freeway entrance to Oakland.

The freeway was jammed with smoldering wrecks of cars, but he drove hard and was able to make his way to the Terminal Freeway exit only to find all traffic almost stopped dead. There were a few openings on the departure road, with people scrambling for the Terminal in any way they could. Many who did not move out to the way fast enough were either run over or shot, or both.

Sam was dodging cars, bullets, and laser blasts but making some progress until he heard Malcolm's voice. "Having a nice drive, Sam?"

Sam looked at Malcolm's face on the monitor. "I'm coming to join you, Malcolm."

"Really, Sam?"

"Yes. You are right. I'm have no claims on Yosemite, and I want to live."

"You're not a very good liar, Sam?"

"You should know. Tell me. Have you ever once – in all the millenniums – told the truth?"

"Yes, I offered the Nazarene the entire world. And he could have had it."

"Stick around. He may have it yet!"

"Turn around and do not come to Yosemite if you care for Tiye!"

"I am not coming for her."

"Oh? So, you have found your Ahwahnechee soul?"

"Not quite yet. I need you to leave Pywiack alone."

"You believe its waters will rid you of your guilt?"

"It's all I want. Just leave it alone."

"Sorry Sam. Can't promise that anything outside my temple will survive."

"Then you leave me no choice. I'll be seeing you soon."

Malcolm put Tiye on camera.

Tiye appeared smiling. "Sam, if you must come, promise you won't interfere, and I will see that you aren't harmed."

Sam found it hard to look at her without a bitter taste in his mouth. "This doesn't concern you. Cut her transmission, Malcolm!"

Malcolm came back on. "You are a fool, Sam. You will not get past any of my roadblocks, so do all a favor and turn around."

"No! I am not a fool. And I do not come alone!"

"Oh?"

"Yes, I come with Tenaya and a host of Ahwahnechee angels!"

"You mean like this?" Malcolm projected a hologram of Tenaya, sitting on his Cayuse pony in full war dress, along with a host of Ahwahnechee angels.

Sam was dumbstruck but forced himself not to reveal his disappointment to Malcolm as he replied. "We will see what is real and what is not, when I get there!":

"Very well. Then do not expect to rely on any friendship favors and expect to die soon." Malcolm cut the transmission.

Sam gripped the Golden Acorn tight and said a silent prayer. As he did, he saw the train begin to move and knew he only had a few minutes to act. He did not know what exactly he would do until he thought of Malcolm bathing in the sacred waters of Pywiack. That thought caused the Black Dog to stir. He had never been so filled with rage. He shook all over and began to growl. As a dozen einsatz gruppe ZZ Goons came after him, he summoned The Black Dog and leaped from the cab. The Goons pulled their weapons, but The Black Dog was on them before they could fire. It tore into them, ripping the throats out of those who did not run.

Soon, Sam was inside the Terminal chock full of people.

They blocked his way to the Departure Gates to Merced until he snarled and tore at a few. Then they parted and opened a pathway he used to lope across the platform toward the train some distance down the tracks. He ran as hard as he could but was not catching up to it. He was at full speed and almost despairing that he could catch it.

Suddenly, he felt a boos t of energy that gave him the strength to run faster. He made one final desperate leap at the last car but fell short. His heart sank when some unseen wind at his back propelled in on top of the previous car, where he lay down exhausted. He was not too tired to praise Tenaya for his help.

Sam was wrong; it was not Tenaya.

Malcolm had watched and knew who it was. "Michael!" He cursed aloud. "You are in rebellion. When will you pay as I have?" There was an eerie silence before loud rolls of thunder boomed out of a cloudless sky, and there was some hell to pay in heaven. It made Satan smile.

CHAPTER EIGHT

The domino theory was proven in the first five seconds of the massive earthquake. The tallest building shifted, buckled, then tumbled into the next tallest, row after row, until nothing was left standing. Everyone had predicted "The Big One" would come eventually. No one had expected the intense rock magnetism and core radiation that would follow. No one predicted that the axial rift would split the Antarctic to the Arctic and East Asia to Somaliland. No one thought that the earth's magnetic core might go wild and generate polarities that made magnetometers a joke on a scale of ten million gammas. No one was so bold as to predict a continental drift that would slam Siberia into Alaska and raise a tidal wave that would destroy the Solomon Islands in fifteen seconds and make American Samoa, a Japanese offshore island.

In Southern California, Steven Lucas surfed the net like the beach boys surfed the ocean waves. He had been arrested at the tender age of thirteen for breaking into the Pentagon computer and threatened with jail if he did it again.

Lately he had been watching Malcolm's saccharine Holocasts and knew he was evil, if not the Anti-Christ. So, Steven believed he might be able to infect Malcolm's systems with a Damascus virus to shut him down.

Through his skill with a computer, he had traveled to outer space, inner space, and inter-dimensional space. He was surrounded by the finest computer equipment that he could make, granted him the most exotic wishes. He had done it all twice, and he was not happy. He wanted to accomplish something worthwhile even though he didn't like this world at all.

Steven had no real friends, and most people thought he was a super-geek.

This day he would get even the score.

The Damascus virus Steven intended to inflict on Malcolm and his tormentors was a thing of beauty to a lover of such subtle destruction as him. With a stroke of his keyboard, he was inside his beloved cyberspace where he was a Superhero and not a geek.

There he could do and be anything he wanted.

He grinned as he thought about the screens going blank all over the world and people staring at them in disbelief. He laughed as he thought of people watching their hearts' desires wiped out in a flash. He cackled as he programmed the virus to strike.

In moments, the monitor told him the virus was in place, and soon he would have his revenge. He could imagine Malcolm and his detractors going mad. Most of all anyone who had mocked would laugh no more. He was pleased with himself and chuckling until his monitor screen went black.

Frantically, he tried to reboot. As he did, his finger became stuck on the "ctrl" button and the monitor screen lit up again.

"A fatal error has occurred!" a sarcastic voice intoned. Seconds later, Steven felt a jolt of electricity shoot through his body, singing his hair and throwing him to the floor. As he lay on the floor, he found he could not move a muscle. He looked up to see Malcolm appear on the monitor screen.

"Since you are a loyal subscriber to Mabius Media you have earned total access to "Malcolm's Holy Hour Of Decision" Holocasts. Please, sit back and relax. They will be broadcast uninterrupted until you cancel your subscription. The first Holocast is only 12 hours long on how to be a good boy in a troubled time." Malcolm appeared in a mega BVR Holocast grinning.

Steven thought you had to die to go to hell.

He was wrong.

He had not died.

* * *

Hoover Dam is the largest free form dam in the world. It dams the Colorado River at a point in Black Canyon at the Nevada-Arizona line. It stands 727 feet high and is 1282 feet long. It supplies all the drinking water and electricity for Las Vegas, the wide-open town that glittered thirty-six miles beneath its billion tons of water.

Mrs. Miller, the proverbial little old lady in tennis shoes, balanced the bucket of coins and pulled the slot machine handles with practiced skill. She was the scourge of the casinos. They hated to see her coming. She had a knack for hitting jackpots no matter how fine the machines were set. She had lost, Harry her beloved husband of fifty years, and all she had to do with her time was pull the slots.

The pit bosses often wondered why her aging arm didn't fall off.

Many wished it would, including Jake Gusage, a part owner. Jake watched as Mrs. Miller hit two jackpots in a row and shook his head in disgust. He moved to see if he could pull her away with an offer of tasty food and luxury rooms. "Mrs. Miller. You look tired. How about a free pass to the buffet and a suite where you can rest up on one of our Heavenly-pedic beds?"

"Oh, no Jake. I'm on a hot streak. Nothing short of an earthquake is going to stop me now. Even that might not!" She laughed.

Jake thought it over. "It's Sunday shouldn't you be in church?"

"Now Jake. You know all the churches have been shut down and boarded up. And it is illegal to pray."

"Look old woman! I tried to be nice. I want you out of here. Understand?"

Mrs. Miller eyed him with a kind smile. "Out of here, like how my husband was run out of here?"

"He was a drunkard and molested the cocktail waitresses."

"Lies to keep him out because he was a winner! You don't like winners do you, Jake?"

"Maybe I do, or I don't. But as far as you are concerned, enough is enough!" Jake pulled the plug on her machine.

Mrs. Miller looked at him and grinned. "That won't stop me, Jake. There are other machines."

"For goodness's sake get a life. Don't you have anything else to do besides sitting here pulling these levers?"

"I guess. But if I stay here long enough Harry will come join me."

"Really? I'd like to see that. Your husband has been dead for a year!"

"No matter. Just wait. He's coming and he wants to talk to you!"

"That's it. You are certifiable. I am calling the white coats and you are going to be put away." Jake stopped as he heard a distant thunder. He was frozen into inaction as he turned to see a hundred-foot wall of water roaring down the canyon. He looked up to see all the other people who had noticed it were fleeing the Casino. He was not able to say another word as the wall of water washed away Las Vegas.

All but Mrs. Miller, who was alone in a gilded Casino sitting before a celestial slot machine. She was soon joined by Harry. She smiled at him with a happy heart, and they shared a sweet kiss. Then she pulled the lever on the slot machine handle and hit three triple Angels on the drums.

CHAPTER NINE

Michael had been warned, and as hard as it would be, he promised not to meddle in fate anymore. Turning his attention away from human foils, he watched as the lion and his friend, the young Ox, enjoyed a bale of hay. Nearby a Mother Bear smiled as her cubs played with a young calf. A porcupine and a skunk playfully wrestled with no harm falling on either. Adults in pristine toned new bodies played silly games, and their laughter was the joyous sound of happy children. All the length and breadth of the heavens could be seen majestic mansions and new fertile lands flowing with crystal waters and forests of trees bearing delicious fruits.

Michael watched as David and Solomon were checking the plans for the Temple to be built in New Jerusalem, and he knew it was a model for the new earth to come. It was wonderful to behold. Yet he thought it was much too good for and more than humans deserved. If he had his way, he would end it all now. He fought off those thoughts and made his anxious heart repeat – God's will be done.

*　*　*

As the train left the Oakland train terminal, Sam lay on top of the last car and looked back across the Bay. San Francisco was now breaking apart, and huge fires lit the horizon. Hordes of people were running down the tracks, and many were trampled, while others threw anything they could pick up at the disappearing train. He felt a little guilty for leaving them behind. Then he cursed himself for any trace of sentiment. They had abused the earth so maybe they had it coming.

Sam vowed that if he saved Ahwahnee he would not allow anyone to enter who did not love it as much as he. Any abuse would be met by instant death. It was an insane thought but seemed logical to his tortured mind. He dismissed that thought and worried that he was becoming too much like Malcolm.

Sam whimpered a little as The Black Dog lay down. Now he had to decide what he would do to stop things. He saw his reflection in the polished steel of the train and sighed hard. He had morphed back to his White Eyes form and wondered if he had ever had any other.

As the train moved along, Sam looked up to see Mosquito. and Gnat drones pass over him. He expected one of them would zap him at any moment.

When they didn't, he wondered why.

He managed to clasp the Necklace around his neck, and as he touched the Golden Acorn, he began to have faith Tenaya would protect him. He was jerked back to reality when the train took a curve at high speed, and he almost slid off the top of the car. At the last moment, he was able to swing himself on the observation platform and fall back safely. He expected to see Facista or einsatz gruppe ZZ Goons, but there were none to be seen, and the drones had disappeared.

"My goodness, that was some acrobatic feat! "A man's voice came out of the shadows.

Sam looked up to see a man dressed in fishing clothes standing by a pile of fishing gear, looking down and smiling at him. He eased to his feet and gathered his thoughts. "What? Who are you?"

My name is James Sam. My friends call me Jim or Jimmy."

"How do you know my name?"

James smiled and shook his head. "Well, anyone who watches any media has seen your pictures."

"Oh!"

"It's amazing you got past all the security. You are a most wanted man, Sam."

"Yeah!…and you. What is this ruse all about, Malcolm?"

"Malcolm? I don't understand."

Sam picked up a fishing rod and held it to James's face! "You're going fishing at Ahwahnee, James?"

"Tenaya!" James replied.

"What did you say?"

"Tenaya Creek. The best Trout fishing in the world."

"Not anymore."

"Oh? You are wrong. My happiest days were fishing there with my Dad. He will meet me there."

Sam saw the joy in the man's eyes and knew he was being scammed by Malcolm. He did not have the heart to tell him that. Sam did have fond memories of Tenaya creek when it was so full of fish, he could catch them with his hands. He smiled and nodded.

Sam pondered Malcolm's proposals. It was clear the world was descending not devastation and maybe Malcolm could bring back Tenaya Creek and all Ahwahnee to its former glory.

Then he stopped to censure himself.

James was just another way of Malcolm's temptations. Sam could barely restrain himself from punching James. But he decided not to rise to Malcolm's bait. "Can I join you and your father?"

James grimaced then grinned."If we leave all to Malcolm and you will have it as it was."

Sam balled his fist and punched at James. His fist hit a group of fading pixels and the disappearing Cheshire grin of James before it hit the metal wall of the train. "Damn you, Malcolm.

This kind of stuff won't save you!"

"Are you okay, sir?" A Robo Lady Steward appeared on the platform and looked at Sam like he was an ogre.

Sam was woozy, but when his eyes cleared, he saw the condescending look on Steward's face with contempt. "O generation of vipers, who hath warned you to flee from the wrath to come?"

"Sir! Would you like to enter the lounge and have a drink?"

"A drink? Firewater to cloud my brain so you can steal our land!"

"Excuse me?"

"Whore of Babylon! Get away from me!"

"Please come in, have a seat and take it easy, sir?"

Sam thought it over and calmed down. "Yes, I would like to come in and have a drink with Malcolm. Think you can arrange that?"

"Malcolm?"

"Come on, cut the B. S. Just go tell your Master I want to talk."

"Malcolm? Yes. I will check on that." She paused to look deadly serious. "Please wait here." She went through a door to the Club Carr and began to close it.

Sam tried to catch it before it closed but it slammed in his face. He shrugged and started to move away. He stopped when he heard the loud sound of cattle car train wheels clicking on the rails. It was not the muffled sound modern rail cars made but the sound of cheap iron wheels on poor quality track. In between the clacks of the wheels, he could hear the moans of people in agony. He grabbed the doorknob and swung it open. As he looked inside, he saw people packed together shoulder to shoulder with nowhere to sit. They stood in sewage up to their ankles and the smell burned his eyes. Their faces ached with hunger, and their tongues were swollen from lack of water. They all turned to him and held out their hands in the hope he was there to save them.

The scene was so horrific he closed the door.

Sam leaned against the closed door until he could stand the moans no longer. He turned and opened the door again to see the interior of a luxury lounge with well-dressed people seated at linen-covered tables eating off fine china. They all looked well fed and were drinking fine wines. The air smelled of Spring Lavender and soft music filled the air. All the passengers paused eating and waved at him to join them. Sam was so jaded by Holographic magic that he almost believed it. It was only a moment before he both admired and hated Malcolm's illusions. "Good people! It's a lie, can't you see it. You all must get off the train now!"

The Passengers looked at him like he was insane. Some seated at tables close to him got up and moved some distance away. "Open your eyes and see that you are surrounded by lies.

Nothing you see is real on this voyage of the damned!"

The lounge was filled with snickers and derisive laughter.

"Wake up! You are surrounded by an ocean of cunning deceit. We must stop this train now!" Sam pulled on the emergency cord; it morphed into a snake that struck at him. He reeled backward and fell into the strong arms of an Ahwahnechee Medicine Man.

The Medicine man was wearing ceremonial skirt of twisted eagle down and a headdress made of magpie feathers. On his shoulders was a tunic adorned with blue tassels, which he shook in Sam's face. Sam was both shocked and pleasantly surprised. "Oh, Thank God. One of my people!"

"I am Ahwahnechee. Who are your people?"

"I...I am...."

"Where is it you go?" The Medicine man snarled.

"I go to save Ahwahnee."

"No! You are not welcome there!"

Sam backed up and looked him over. "OK. Malcolm enough! You are going to have to kill me to stop me from going to Ahwahnee!" Everyone in the lounge broke into derisive laughter.

Sam covered his ears and grimaced in pain. His head hurt so much that he closed his eyes. When he opened them, he saw The Medicine Man was gone, and John Pattos was standing in front of him.

"He will kill you, Sam. We do not want that." John pleaded.

Sam laughed a deeply cynical laugh. "Where is Malcolm – your Lord and Master? I want to see him now!"

"Sam, you do not want to provoke him any further. Can I ask as a friend that you get off the train at the first stop and do not come to Yosemite?"

"Ask all you want. It won't happen."

"So, you wish Tiye to be harmed?"

Sam was taken by the serious look in John's eyes. "No! I do not..."

"She is risking her life to save you stubborn self!"

Sam sensed Joh was telling the truth until he noticed redness on top of John's right hand. He knew he didn't have to see Malcolm. Since John was implanted, he was talking to him now. "You know John. Maybe you are right. It's most probably better for all if I don't come to Yosemite." Sam stopped to smile. "Just ask Malcolm if I can talk to Tiye first."

John looked doubtful, then nodded. "I will see if that is possible." John turned to go.

"John?" Sam called after him.

John turned back. "Yes, Sam?"

"What called you to become a Priest?"

John was stunned by the question for a moment. "I...I...am not a Priest."

"You were one once."

John's eyes revealed pain as he thought it over.

"I am just curious how a person knows if they are called by God or by some false prophet?" Sam probed.

John winced as he felt a pain in his right hand. A small tear formed in the corner of both eyes.

"I mean; why did you leave your calling? Did you steal the poor box?" Sam half-joked.

"No! Heresy."

"I thought that went out with fish on Friday."

"*Nuestra Señora de la Santa Muerte.*"

"Say what?"

"I ministered to members of my congregation devoted to her. It was a parish in a barrio. They were mostly the desperately poor, gays, night workers, and others of the dispossessed who gained comfort from prayers to her."

"*Muerte?* Isn't that death in Spanish?"

"Yes. However, she holds a scythe, not to reap the dead but to harvest hope. The big boys didn't like that." John shook his head sadly.

"Now there is why I say religion sucks!"

"Perhaps you mean some religious practices."

"What's the difference?"

"You may not belong to a religion, Sam. But I'll bet you have religious practices."

"Like what?"

"Oh, everyone has a prayer of some kind to something other than themselves."

"You mean no atheists in foxholes thing?" "Precisely."

"Okay, I'll admit to the belief in the spirit of the earth and the sacred waters of Ahwahnee."

"Please do not go there, Sam!"

"Tell you what. Go get Malcolm and tell him I want to talk about it."

John nodded.

"Also, tell Ty, I need to talk to her."

"I beg you to leave her be. She is the only reason you are not dead." John insisted with serious eyes before he turned and walked off.

John's words rang true, and Sam felt a moral weakness he had never felt before. It was all piling up on his psyche, and he felt cracks appearing in his iron will. He chuckled a cynical chuckle. He suspected he was now pathologically insane. If he had a gun, he would rejoice in ending it all quick. He wished he could tear his brain from his body and squash it until all the pain was gone. He looked up to see a BVR Steward serving drinks at a bar. He got up and ran to it. He grabbed two handfuls of mini bottles of vodka and gulped three down before the BVR Steward could react.

"More! More!" Sam leaped over the bar and picked up a liter bottle and began to chug it. When the bottle was empty, he was stunned that the vodka had no effect. His spirit was stuck in a morass of muddled spiritualism, and The Black Dog was stirring. Sam watched as his hands trembled. He grimaced as he felt painful muscle spasms. His head hurt with a migraine headache that caused near blindness – a fifth star formed on his right hand.

Sam looked at it with indifference, and then he was compelled to bark like a junkyard dog.

The other passengers jammed up against each other as they backed away. Sam howled as he got up and moved to a window. He leaned his face against the window and looked back toward San

Francisco. Intense pain tried to force tears he would not allow. "Ty! I need you, Ty! Oh, God! I need you!" With misty eyes, Sam watched the distant glow of the raging fire that had been San Francisco. He clenched his fists.

He hurt and let the Black Dog lie down.

"My goodness, Sam! What strange hell have you descended to?" familiar voice echoed around him.

Sam looked up to see Malcolm morphed into a young Donavan holding Tiye's hand. They were both smiling down at him.

Sam was too weak to react for a few moments before he struggled to his feet. "Ty?"

"Sam, I begged you not to come." Tiye seemed sympathetic.

"Donavan?" Sam grimaced as he looked Donavan over.

"It's what Ty wanted, and I always strive to please the ladies," Malcolm replied as he put his arm around Tiye.

Tiye snuggled close to him and seemed happy.

Sam steadied himself and looked them over. "No! Just another lie, Malcolm. When do they all end?"

"For you, they have ended, my friend. I have no more patience for your interferences. I offered friendship and paradise. You refused both, and so you will have neither." Donavan morphed back to Malcolm.

Sam looked at Tiye for some sign she was on his side.

Tiye turned away and whispered something in Malcolm's ear. Malcolm smiled and nodded, then looked at Sam with a hint of sadness before he looked stern. "I will give you a few moments to say goodbyes," Malcolm said, then turned and walked away.

Sam and Tiye stood quietly looking at each other for a few moments after Malcolm was gone. Sam ached to reach out and take her into his arms, but there was a deep invisible chill between them now, and he could just as easily strangle her.

"Please, Sam. Just listen to reason. Give up your foolish quest. Pledge yourself to his service, and he will spare you."

"Donavan, Ty?"

"Forget that. Just try not to be your stubborn self. He will kill you – or worse – implant you with the new Chip that has a painful death feature if removed."

"A Hobson's choice."

"No, a sane realistic choice."

"You wish me to betray my mother and the Great Spirit?"

"It wasn't your mother, or Tenaya, Sam. There are no spirits. All you have seen are the latest Holographic Projections Malcolm wanted to test out on you."

"You mean, I won't be fishing in Tanaya creek?"

"In time. If you allow Malcolm to restore it."

Sam took her hands and looked them over, There was no sign of an implant. He was almost brought to his knees by the realization she was lost to him. "You do this of your own free will?"

"Yes."

Sam toyed with The Golden Acorn. "Then this has no power."

"I'm afraid not. You will have no protection – even if you can make it there."

Sam unclasped the necklace and held it out to her. "Take it and remember me."

Tiye started to take it but held back.

Sam looked suspicious. "It's just a trinket, right?"

Tiye smiled then took it.

Sam looked at her hands, and they were not burned. She put it around her neck and clasped it. It looked like it belonged there and seemed to enhance her beauty.

It also chilled Sam's faith in all he believed.

"It is beautiful. Thank you, Sam."

"It looks good on you, but I don't think, Donava...Malcolm will like it."

"We do what we must to survive." Tiye's words were laden with caution, yet in them was a whisper of love.

Sam was a psychological mess.

The Black Dog wanted to tear into her. His heart restrained. it in the hope she might have sacrificed much for him and was in mortal danger. He also knew he could not yield his soul to Malcolm.

Somehow, he knew that all that stood between him, and perdition was not to turn his back on his ancestors and the Great Spirit. His visions of Tenaya were not Holograms. He sensed they were real. But his will was tossed in an emotional storm on a raging sea of conflicts. He had to hold on to his tiny raft of belief even though a huge wave of doubt threatened to drown him. Ironically, his only hope was to out lie the great liar. "Tell, Malcolm; I will be glad to be part of his congregation." Sam offered.

Tiye looked at him. She knew he was not being truthful, but she would play it out. "I'll go tell him." she smiled, touched his cheek with a gentle hand, then turned and walked away.

Sam watched her go, and his resolve began to weaken.

Maybe what he wanted for himself would endanger her life, and he would be the cause of her death. He felt a sudden rush of weariness and plopped down on a Luxurious couch seat. As he lay back, he thought he heard the clack of old iron on cheap rails. The sound passed and he fell into a deep sleep.

CHAPTER TEN

Sam was soaked with perspiration as he visualized Tiye trapped in the fiery rubble of San Francisco. "No! No! No!" He struggled to awaken.

"Are you okay?" Tiye's voice soothed.

Sam looked up to see Tiye's smiling face. "I had a crazy dream."

"The docs gave you a calmative. You needed rest."

"You got that right." Sam looked around. "Where is our benevolent benefactor?"

"He is busy with some things."

"So, I'm in the club?"

"Sort of. Let's say – on probation."

Sam started to object but nodded. "I guess that's fair."

"There is a lot at stake, Sam. Just try to keep that in mind."

"I am on board just so long as you promise, no more BVR Holocasts, CGI, Ghosts, or more tricks. Please!"

"Of course. It will all be real, and you will love it."

"I promise to be a good boy." He smiled. "So, what's our next move?"

"I have convinced Malcolm to let you off at the Merced Terminal. You cannot board the Yart shuttle."

"You mean I can't go to Yosemite." "You said, Yosemite."

"Like a good little soldier."

"I hope so. Anyway, you will be quartered at a Refugee Camp for just a few days before you join us in Yosemite."

"Refugee Camp?"

"Yes. Please just go along with things for a while. Okay?"

Sam nodded and thought it over. "Didn't you say the new Holograms are so good even you can't tell if they are not real?"

"Yes! They are…" Tiye was interrupted by Sam pulling her down on his lips and kissing her enthusiastically. He broke the kiss and sighed hard. "Yes! Real!"

Tiye smiled, but her eyes were full of pain. "I can't, Sam."

"Can't what."

"We can't be us anymore." Tiye's eyes revealed hurt before she could stop it.

Sam stepped back and thought it over. "Orders from headquarters?"

"Can you just trust me?"

"You made some kind of deal?"

"You didn't answer me."

"Oh? Can I trust you? Let's just say you are on probation!"

"Wake up, Sam! You are not in control here! I risked a lot to save your crazy ass!" Tiye snapped.

Sam turned and looked at a red glow reflected in the train's window. He watched it flicker and looked sad before he sighed hard. "San Francisco. It's gone. All gone."

"I guess you're waiting for me to say you were right?" Tiye followed his eyes.

"I take no delight in it."

Tiye looked doubtful. She sat back in her seat and grimaced. "You were right."

Sam looked at her with love. "That wasn't necessary." "They are saying this is all caused by the San Andreas fault collapsing."

"And if I said it is not following the fault line?"

Tiye studied the hurt in his tired eyes. "I would listen to the learned geologist!"

"Flattery will get you anything you want."

Tiye looked dead serious. "A promise not to come to Yosemite."

"I'll be an obedient servant and stay at this so-called 'Refugee Camp' until it's ok to come. Okay?"

"No! I mean never."

"I can't promise that…"

"Just don't come. Can you give me that promise for all I have done?"

Sam sighed a long hard, sad sigh. "I wish I could, my love."

"Then you will die there! You, stubborn digger!"

"What did you call me?"

"I am trying to get through that thick skull of yours!"

"Don't ever say that to me again."

"Bye, Sam. I tried."

"For Donavan or for me?"

"If you have to ask that, there is nothing else for us to say."

Sam was about to reply when the loud clack of old iron on worn rails echoed around them.

"Listen! Did you hear that?"

Tiye shook her head.

Sam looked for a hint of deceit in her eyes. He saw none. "This is no first-class train car. It's cattle car transport. Listen." They fell silent.

Tiye seemed to listen, but no sound was heard. She slowly began to back away from him.

"I'm not crazy, Ty. Even though you and his legions have spared no ruse to make me that way.'

"Then, you are going to Yosemite?"

"Yes." Sam paused and grinned. "Hell yes!"

"And what can you possibly do if you do go there?"

"I expect the spirts will guide me."

"How can you believe anything you see?"

"I see things more clearly there. "Sam stopped and shrugged. "And if I don't, that is where I wish to die. Not in a Merced Train Terminal or Refuge Camp!"

Tiye could not help but smile at him. "How? How will you get past his security?"

"Malcolm will let me." Sam spoke to the air. "He wants me to lead him to a particular tree – don't you, Malcolm?"

"What are you talking about, Sam?'

"He's listening, and he knows." Sam grinned. "Listen up, Malcolm. Call off your goons, and I will find your tree."

"One tree in all of Yosemite?" Tiye scoffed.

"I'll start with Mariposa grove. Ok, Malcolm?"

"Mariposa Grove. Why there?"

"Many years ago, I planted a magic acorn in Mariposa Grove. By now, it's a full-grown Black Oak."

"Acorns are not magic, Sam."

"What is more magic than a tiny acorn growing into a mighty oak?"

Tiye had to nod.

"That's my deal. Take it or leave it, Malcolm." Sam fell silent as if waiting for an answer.

Tiye looked doubtful. "You mean to do this, no matter what, Sam?"

"Yes. And I will ignore any holograms of any kind trying to guilt-trip me into not doing it. Ok?" He reached out to caress her face with a soft touch of his fingers.

Tiye avoided his touch as she took off the necklace. A quiet look of understanding passed between them before she handed the necklace with the Golden Acorn back to him. "You might need this."

Sam took it and smiled. "Will I see you again after we leave the train?" Sam almost reached out for her.

Tiye responded with a look of affection, then sadness. "If you hope to find your tree, you'd better hurry, Sam!"

"Why?"

"Because they are clear-cutting Mariposa Grove," Tiye said with a look of mock sympathy.

CHAPTER ELEVEN

Parts of the earth's crust were now moving at a measurable speed of three miles an hour. As a result of melting icebergs, the North Sea off the British coast undulated Bristol and was well on its way to flooding London. The South Atlantic seaboard began to slide into the ocean, and Coastal cities from Miami to Cape Hatteras were swallowed up by deep- sea sediments. The Appalachian Mountains were inching closer and closer toward the heartland except for a small area between the North American cretaceous paleolatitudes. Meteorology, never an exact science, became a dead science as temperatures fluctuated wildly in all geographical areas. The world's hot spot at a given moment was Siberia, and its cold spot Blythe, California. In Des Moines, people died of heatstroke, clothed in winter garb to protect against the snow. Snow suddenly vanished and left them standing in fur coats in blazing sunlight that reached 150 degrees.

It was not uncommon to p e op l e t o freeze to death below the waist while suffering burn blisters on the upper torso. In the Canadian Arctic Circle, farmers froze to death in t-shirts and overalls, having stripped off their clothes against a burning sun that turned into a howling snowstorm in minutes.

In Chicago, people were pelted with hailstones as big as bowling balls. Lake Michigan's forty feet of lake bottom sludge swallowed most of the city. As if located in the eye of a hurricane, the Yokohama Cubs continued a day game because Wrigley Field stood while buildings all around it crumbled and fell. In Malibu, what was once an offshore reef, washed ashore, crushing the fancy beach houses beneath its jagged coral edges. In the shadow of the flagstaff at the South Pole, in the middle of an ice field a grove of willows appeared. Five minutes South, a bright green meadow spread where the ice flows had once dominated.

In Southwest Africa, the Kilimanjaro glacier slid down onto the Serengeti Plain, crushing animal and human life indiscriminately as it inched toward the sea.

There was no season in its time but a variety of seasons at any given moment.

A person might experience a change of seasons in a flash and find themselves in woolen Parkas in the middle of a heatwave. Rigid laws that applied to longitudes and latitudes were so many lines on the geographer's paper.

Malcolm knew God was getting the earth ready for a ritual bath of blood, and the End times would come soon. He still believed he had time to upset the Nazarene's timetable, and there would be no judgment day except his.

Right now, he was angry that his train Hologram was experiencing glitches. "Who is responsible for the sound leakage on that last projection?" Malcolm yelled at Amon and Oskar. Amon and Oskar backed away in fear shaking their heads.

"Maybe Sam lied and didn't hear or see anything, Master." Oskar sputtered.

"He heard it and saw it! And he'd better not hear or see it again!"

Amon and Oscar wilted and backed away in fear.

Malcolm waited and enjoyed their misery before he cracked a crocodile smile. "Now! Did you find that security camera footage I asked for?"

"Yes, Master. Punch in 66.6 on the main monitor for a playback. Malcolm thought it over as he went to a monitor and punched in the numbers. Moments later he saw a playback of the incident with Sam on the roof:

"How absurd! Let the holy Joe jump. Maybe his prayers will be heard." Malcolm cackled.

Sam sighed hard and smiled before he reached out his hand to Malcolm. "You win. No hard feelings."

Malcolm held back and studied Sam's face, then shrugged and shook Sam's hand. As he did, Sam jerked him into an embrace and pulled them both off the roof.

Amon looked on in shock before he ran to the edge and looked down to see Malcolm hanging onto a ledge. He quickly reached down and helped Malcolm back up. "Good move, Master! He is surely dead, and we are rid of him."

Malcolm glared at Amon, pushed by him, and looked down. There was a thick fog, and little could be seen. Then, through a small break in the fog, Malcolm saw a Pale Horse, whose rider wore the face of Death. He smiled for a moment before he saw the tip of an Archangel's wing disappear into the mist. "No! No! No!"

Malcolm paused the playback and zoomed in on the Angel's wing. As the image got larger, he could also see the handle on the Sword of the Word. He angrily switched off the monitor. "I knew it! Michael is helping and he must be in rebellion. Why is he not cast down!"

"You're right. Sam is getting help." Tiye said as she walked in.

"That's why we should stop playing with him and just kill him, Master." Oskar fumed.

"Shut up." Malcolm glared at him, then turned to greet Tiye with a smile. "We will have no regrets now that Sam has been given every chance. Right?"

"You promised safe passage to Merced."

"And you can see to it. Put him at ease. But he does not enter the gates of Yosemite. Understood?"

Tiye nodded "You have sound leakage on the train Holocast."

"I know it will be fixed."

"I am not comfortable with what you are doing to the Keepers, Malcolm."

"It was the only way to transport so many with limited resources."

"They are to be safe once inside the temple?"

"Yes. You have my word."

Tiye looked at him steeped in guilt and doubt. Two emotions she had tried all her life to avoid. "Yes. If you forgive my doubts – is it ok to stay by Sam until we reach Merced."

"Of course. As I said. Put him at ease. And tell him I wish him well."

"What is this about a tree?"

"A tree? I don't understand?"

"Okay. If that is the way you want it." Tiye half-smiled before she left to go to Sam.

Malcolm grimaced.

Sam had fallen into a deep sleep and grimaced in agony as he endured a horrible nightmare. In his sweat-soaked dream, he was in a crowded Güterwagen box car meant to hold 50 people packed with almost 200. Everyone was struggling to breathe and fighting to get a place by a small, barred window where they would gasp for a small breath of air. No food or water was supplied, and there was only an overflowing bucket latrine for all. Many died on their feet, unable to find a place to fall. Sam was boxed in by people who had died in agony, and they looked at him with accusatory eyes that never blinked.

Tiye was now back to check on him and watched him fidget with his nightmare that caused him to growl and suffer fits of howling. She feared the Black Dog might be waking but thought it might be less dangerous than letting him play the nightmares out. Her thoughts were interrupted by a statuesque Robo Steward trying to wake Sam.

"I wouldn't do that!" Tiye said.

"I have to, we are pulling into the station, and he is to be arrested upon arrival."

"What?"

"Those are our orders."

"From whom?"

"Look! I'm just a Steward."

"Well go back and tell whoever gave you those orders to forget it. I will escort him to the Refugee camp."

"Refugee camp?"

"Yes"

The Robo Steward uttered a guttural electronic chuckle.

Tiye knew there was no such camp. She was about to go to Malcolm when Sam awoke in fits and started growling. He snarled at the Robo Steward.

The Robo Steward sputtered and almost shorted out, before she eased away, then turned and ran.

Sam looked up at Tiye. "I was having a terrible nightmare."

"I know. Are you okay?"

"Yeah! Aaahhhmm...I need some cold water." Sam started to get up.

Tiye motioned for him to sit down. "I'll get it."

Sam thought it over and nodded.

"I'll be right back." Tiye turned to leave.

Sam got up and started to follow. He stopped when he felt a hand on his shoulder.

"Bad nightmare, Sam?"

Sam looked up to see John. "Padre?"

"John."

"John! Your people! Warn them now! This is not a passenger train. It's a *Deutsche Reichsbahn* cattle car.

"No, Sam. You had a bad dream." John soothed.

"I heard the clack of the old wheels. I saw..."

"It all in a nightmare, Sam. Look around at the first-class setting. It was just a dream."

Sam saw the well-dressed people laughing, sipping cocktails and fine wine while dining on gourmet food. He knew deep down not to believe his eyes, yet he also worried about pressing his sanity any further. "It's all illusion." Sam sighed for strength. "Isn't it?"

"No, Sam, you must get past your suspicions and realize Malcolm is saving us all."

Sam was fully awake and filled with anger. "When are you going to wake up and smell the brimstone?"

"I know of your doubts. I have had them also. I am sure you will understand it all in time."

Sam thought it over and smiled. "Maybe you are right. Can I ask you something, Padre?"

"John, please. And ask away."

"Yes. John!' Sam paused to break a pleasant smile. "So, John tell me about Revelations Chapter Twenty."

John was stunned for a moment then shrugged. "What about it?"

"*Then I saw an angel coming down from heaven, holding the key of the abyss and a great chain in his hand. And he laid hold of the dragon, the serpent of old, who is the devil and Satan, and bound him for a thousand years; and he threw him into the abyss and shut it and sealed it over him.*" Sam quoted.

"You have a scholar's knowledge of scripture."

"Tell me, John. If you were Satan, what would you do to avoid that?"

John eased away nervously. "Some say Revelations is a Christian myth written by a crazy man."

"Yes. Depending on your point of view, John, the Divine, was a prophet or insane." Sam agreed, then looked deadly serious. "What if it isn't myth? Come on, John! Even a blind man can heed the signs of the times."

"Revelations doesn't say anything others haven't predicted. The Hindus believe the end time will come when Kalki descends atop a white horse. The Buddhists believe a Bodhisattva named Maitreya will appear, and the destruction of the world will then come through the seven suns. There are many…"

"Seven? Suns?" Sam stopped him.

"Yes. It's mythical, Sam."

"No, it isn't. Seven suns? Seven churches. Seven super volcanoes, erupting at once," Sam mumbled.

"No, Sam. That's a geologic impossibility."

"Yes, but not a nuclear impossibility."

"Sam, I think your nightmare has you a little off balance. Why don't you…"

"Whoa! How diabolical. Padre, if you were God, where would you want your throne on earth to be?"

"I don't know. Why?"

"A prophecy from Thessalonians about thrones and pretending to be God." Sam looked deadly serious. "We can't let it happen."

"I will pray you get well, Sam."

"Oh, I am quite well, Padre. My eyes are wide open now. Malcolm as Mochni the bird, has made people hate instead of loving each other. We should have learned from the ant people and obeyed the plan of creation?"

"You are well-read, Sam."

"Comparative Religion 101."

"So, you are a believer after all?"

"I didn't say that, but if you see a rider on a Pale Horse dressed in the morbid hoods of death trailing hellfire, run."

John flinched and looked worried. "You have seen such a horseman?"

"Maybe?"

"Did he tell you to look for something – a tree perhaps?"

Before Sam could reply, the train jerked, and Sam turned and took a quick peek out of a window. There was a fog of smoke from fires still burning to the North. Yet as the train pulled into the Merced Terminal, the sky was clear, and it seemed the gateway to Yosemite was unharmed. He turned back and eyed John with suspicion. "Yes, and he told me to protect it with my life, Malcolm!"

John morphed into Malcolm and stood before him, grinning. He looked at the Golden Acorn. "I see she gave it back to you!"

"Yes, Donavan. She did."

"Oh? Donavan was all last night. Today I'm just your old pal, Malcolm."

Sam resisted the urge to punch Malcolm as he stood up and smiled. "You did take me in and for that I owe you. But I don't think we were ever friends."

"Well think what you like. We have arrived at the Terminal and there is transport waiting to take you to a rest camp." Malcolm paused to look serious. "I hope you will go along peacefully, Sam."

Sam could resist it no longer. He reared back and punched Malcolm hard in the chin.

Malcolm reeled back slightly but did not seem to feel it. "My patience is at an end with you. I have no choice but to have you implanted with the new obedience chip. I advise you not to remove it. It will mean an instant painful death." He grinned. "I would not want that for – my friend."

Sam moved to punch him again.

Malcolm motioned for Amon to join them.

Amon came flanked by two einsatz gruppe ZZ Goons, his gun at the ready and a crocodile grin on his face.

"He is to be sent to lock up in Camp Byar and implanted. If he escapes, I need not tell you the penalty you will receive." Malcolm ordered.

"Yes, Master! I will see to…" Amon did not get to finish before Sam punched him in the middle of his grin, sending him to the floor.

The Two ZZ Goons grabbed Sam's arms and restrained him.

Amon got to his feet, wiped the blood from his chin then punched Sam hard.

Sam fell to his knees, and Amon kicked him in the gut. Sam doubled over in pain. He was hurting badly, and it got worse when he looked up to see Tiye joining Malcolm. He glared at Tiye and hoped to see remorse in her eyes. There was none. Instead, she stood by Malcolm and seemed to lend him support. The physical pain was nothing compared to the pain of betrayal.

Amon started to kick Sam again.

Malcolm motioned for him to back off. "We will be going now, Sam. When you think about me, remember I gave you many opportunities to be part of New Eden. You turned your back on all that. Goodbye." Malcolm said as he took Tiye's hand and turned to leave.

Sam looked at Tiye to say something. She gave him a quick smile, then turned and walked away, hand in hand, with Malcolm.

When they were out of sight, Amon glared at Sam and motioned for the two ZZ Goons to restrain Sam's arms. Once Sam was in their grip, Amon began to punch Sam hard, cackling with delight in between each punch.

Sam tried to gather his strength and called on the Black Dog, hoping it would come in all its fury so he could tear them both apart. It did not come until he saw Malcolm and Tiye stop at the exit door. Malcolm morphed to Donavan and shared a long kiss with Tiye.

Amon was about to swing at Sam again when The Black Dog came forth in snarls of righteous anger. The two ZZ Goons aimed their Lasers at him. The Black Dog brought them both down with a single leap ripping away their throats and gobbling down their ZZ insignia.

The Black Dog howled in victory before looking up to see Malcolm and Tiye move out of the car and close the metal door behind them. He ran hard toward the door, leaped, and slammed hard against it. For a moment, he was stunned, and The Black Dog lay down. As he lay there, he felt the Train jolt to a stop at The Merced Terminal.

Once the train was still again, Sam looked up to see Amon smiling down at him holding an Inject-Jet. Before Sam could react, Amon injected the new Chip into Sam's right hand. Sam called for The Black Dog. It whimpered. He got to his feet in anger and was about to punch Amon, when he felt his anger ebb and a strange feeling of love for Satan caused him to smile.

The Fifth Seal

"And when he had opened the fifth seal, I saw under the altar the souls of them that were slain for the word of God, and for the testimony which they held. And they cried with a loud voice, saying, how long, O Lord, holy and true, dost thou not judge and avenge our blood on them that dwell on the earth? And white robes were given unto every one of them; and it was said unto them, that they should rest yet for a little season until their fellow servants also, and their brethren, that should be killed as they should be fulfilled."

CHAPTER TWELVE

Sam was unsure of who he was as he stepped off the train onto the Merced Terminal platform. The night was unseasonably warm, but he was pleased to see that the sky was clear, and the ground was still. He smiled with admiration when he saw what Malcolm had done to a small-town train terminal.

Malcolm had turned the Merced Terminal into a huge Holocast projection room. Instead of the cold beige walls of a normal terminal, the walls were alive with realistic images of flowered meadows, cascading waterfalls, and azure surf bounding against pristine beaches. One projection of Big Sur was so realistic people enjoyed a virtual romp on the sands. At the entrances, waiting to greet the passengers departing the train, were megaBVR "Apostle" figures, handing out food and drink along with verbal and hand-signed blessings. "Welcome to Merced, the gateway to the Rapture! Please move along to the Yart Tram, which will take you to Yosemite." An attendant dressed as a biblical prophet announced.

Sam could see a sign over the exit door that read: "Gateway to Freedom! Welcome to the Chosen Few!" He noticed the baggage screeners were on, but the full-body Compton devices were turned off. There was an electronic counter that registered each person that passed through the detector. The number read "143,999." Just outside the exit was a long luxurious tram that was being loaded with the passengers, who were all smiling as they got aboard. Sam saw one of them was John. He smiled as he now understood that John was right. Malcolm's way was the only way. "Hi, John. Nice to see you."

John turned and looked at him with sadness before he broke into a pleasant smile. "Hello, Sam. So glad you will be joining us.

"No. I don't belong there. I think Malcolm has things for me to do here."

John could barely hide his disappointment. "Camp Byar?"

"Wherever he decides I can best be of service."

"…yes…"

"Have you seen, Ty?"

"She…is not…among my flock."

Sam looked across the terminal to the exit gates. As he did, he felt an urge to touch the Golden Acorn and saw ZZ Obersturmbannführer Rudolf Höss asking some questions, then pointing people in different directions. Old or disabled went one way and healthy people the other.

"Selection?"

"What, Sam?"

"Not screening. It's selection."

"Selection?"

"Yes. The Oskar Stangl kind."

"Selection? No, Sam. You are wrong. Those chosen are going to worship in their new Tabernacle."

"No…I…" Sam felt pain that sent him to his knees.

"Are you okay, Sam?"

Sam slowly got to his feet and looked at John with pain in his eyes.

"What did you see, Sam?"

"I…saw happy people…happy…happy people…"

John looked around to see if they were alone before he replied. "Keep the faith, Sam!"

"Faith? What are you saying, John?"

John grimaced. then took an obsidian knife from his clothing and handed it to Sam. "You are chosen. Do not abandon us." John looked past Sam and saw Amon approaching. "God bless Malcolm, Sam. He has fixed it, so we will all be together at the rapture. We are so happy you are with us now, Sam." John said then scurried away.

Sam watched him go and felt compelled to toss the knife away. Instead, he hid it inside his clothing.

"So glad you could come, Sam!" Amon's voice broke into Sam's thoughts.

Sam turned to see Amon flanked by my two ZZ Goons. Both of Amon's eyes were black and swollen, but not enough to hide the vicious hatred he had for Sam.

"Good to see you, Amon." Sam smiled but felt a growling in his gut.

"What did you tell John?" Amon demanded.

"That I am happy to be here."

"That's all?" Amon tapped a button on a remote device and Sam went to his knees in pain.

"No! Please. I...thought I saw...something."

"You still see it?"

"No! No! Please!" Sam was in agony.

Amon enjoyed Sam's agony for a few moments before he tapped the remote and Sam looked relieved. "That is pain at the lowest setting. If you have any more visions, you will feel pain you can't imagine."

Sam was woozy, but when his vision cleared, he looked up to see Tiye walk up.

"You okay, Sam?" Tiye asked.

Sam wobbled to his feet. "I...I..."

Tiye turned to Amon. "Put that IPI (remote pain injector) away and leave us now!"

"What? I don't take orders from you?"

Tiye held up an MPP (Mega Pixel) Phone that displayed a micro Holocast of Malcolm. "Follow her orders as if they were mine!" Malcolm snapped.

"Yes, Master." Amon grunted.

Tiye turned off the MPP and glared at Amon.

Amon fumed and hesitated before he and the ZZ Goons left.

Tiye waited until Amon and the two Goons were gone before she spoke. "I'm sorry he caused you pain."

Sam looked at her and wanted to hold her, but his arms would not move. He felt some pain and backed away. "You belong to Donavan. We must not touch."

Tiye did not like seeing him like this. She felt guilty that she was partially to blame and felt the urge to walk away. She dismissed that thought and wondered, that perhaps, it was time to stop running away. "I need the necklace, Sam" Tiye said in a commanding voice that compelled him to obey.

"Yes! Of course." Sam reached to unclasp it and it burned his fingers. "I don't understand." Sam tried again and it burned his fingers more. He looked at his hands and at Tiye.

"You have to take it off, Ty."

Tiye hesitated, then touched the necklace. It burned her fingers also.

"It is but a trinket, no?" Sam asked.

Tiye was thinking it over when Amon returned.

"I have this, Amon. I told you to go!" Tiye insisted.

Amon held up his MPP and projected Malcolm.

"Let Amon handle it now!" Malcolm ordered.

Amon turned off the MPP and glared at Tiye. "Now go. Woman!"

Tiye and Amon exchanged hateful glances before she looked at Sam with kind eyes tinged with hurt, then turned and walked away.

Sam watched as Tiye passed through the exit. As she did, she was transformed into a woman with a shaved head wearing rags. She looked back at him in pain, with tears in her eyes, as the digital counter at the gate clicked over to read: 144,000.

Sam pushed Amon aside and started to go to her. "Get out of my way, Amon!"

Amon punched the remote and Sam felt pain that brought him to his knees. As he went down the obsidian knife fell out of his clothes.

Amon stared to pick it up, but Sam grabbed it first.

Amon punched up so much pain that Sam almost dropped it. He grimaced as he fought off the pain and drove the knife into the implant site.

"Go ahead crazy man. It will be fun to watch you die in agony" Amon chortled.

Sam hesitated only a moment before he cut the Chip out and it fell to the floor. Both he and Amon were shocked when Sam did not die but seemed to have renewed strength.

Amon pulled a gun and aimed to fire. Just as he was about to pull the trigger, Sam bolted past him and took off running, darting into a large crowd of people.

Amon held his fire as Sam disappeared into the crowd.

Sam ducked around passageways and when he was out of Amon's sight, ran after the Yart Tram. He was almost to the Tram before it picked up speed and pulled away from him; he fell as he reached for it. When he looked up, he could see Tiye looking out a window with a look of desperation on her face. Was it the real Tiye or a Holographic lure of Malcolm's? He was about to go after her, when a bullet from Amon's Walther P38 whizzed by his ear, and Laser Blasts from three ZZ Goons peppered the ground around him.

Sam looked around and saw a Humvee a few feet away. He broke into a run dodging stray shots and made it to the driver's side door. He opened it and sighed in relief to see the keys in the ignition. He leaped in the passenger seat, then got behind the wheel and started the motor.

As Sam drove off, bullets began to pepper the Humvee. They made loud pings but had no impact. He sighed in relief that he had found an armor-kitted Humvee. His relief was short-lived when he looked in his rear-view mirror to see a squad of ZZ Goons kneel in a firing position. Each of them had an armor-piercing PG-7V26 on their shoulder and were ready to fire.

The Tram was just a little distance away from him as he gunned the engine and drove. A rocket zoomed past him and exploded 30 yards ahead. Another zoomed off into the night and exploded even closer. The force of the explosions rocked the Humvee, but Sam could steady it. He was now only a few yards behind the tram when he looked up to see a naked man wearing only a Kipah running toward him and pulling his half-naked wife behind him.

Sam had to hit the brakes hard and almost rolled over, avoiding the man. When he came to a stop, he looked back at the man running toward him.

"No! No! No! It is a lie. Run! Run for your lives! They are selecting us for…." The man was shot dead by bullets from Amon's Walther P38 before he could finish. His wife gasped in shock just before she was gunned down also.

Sam gripped the steering wheel tight and began making swerving motions to avoid the shooting. He saw one ZZ Goon ready to fire a rocket that would blow him away. He veered so much he almost overturned. When he was upright again, he was surprised to see the ZZ Goon had lowered the rocket and the shooting had stopped. He looked into the side-view mirror to see a smug Malcolm motioning for the ZZ Goons to lower their weapons.

The ZZ Goons complied with a Nazi salute.

Malcolm waved at Sam.

Sam grimaced and flipped him the bird.

"I'm sorry, Boss." Amon cowered beside Malcolm.

"For?"

"Letting him escape."

"So?"

"You said you thought the necklace was real and he was being helped by Indian spirits."

"Yes. I hope he is."

"I don't understand."

"You don't need to. Just watch his every move and see where he leads us."

"He cut the chip out, so how can we track him."

"The chip is around his neck!"

"Oh? Good move, Master."

Malcolm shrugged then looked serious. "What time is it?"

"Aaahhmmm! 4:46 PST."

"Not that time. The real-time!"
"Oh? Last I checked, it read, 11:59:55."
Satan shivered.

CHAPTER THIRTEEN

The many mansions of Heaven all sit upon estate grounds that are pristine worlds all their own. They are as grand and lofty or rustic and humble as the blessed soul desires. Some prefer an endless wilderness full of new discoveries. Others want a dock extending into a crystal sea. A few like the tranquility of a desert with a welcoming oasis. No matter where it is located, the air is as sweet each day as if it had rained all night. Lush lawns filled with lions romping with lambs, scented Gardens and huge stands of redwoods abound. Even lovers of precious metals leave their gold laid out as no thieves may break through or steal.

In God's house, all these mansions await the faithful.

As Michael looked upon them, he felt some were better than his and that they were all much too good for humans.

* * *

Yosemite was Malcolm's AI generated megaBVR Holographic Production of a New Eden. Sam had driven back trails he hoped not even Tiye knew and now stood on top of El Capitan looking down at Malcolm's creation. In the brief time he had been gone, Malcolm had erected a twenty-foot wall that encircled most of the meadow. Holographic projectors filled one wall with a detailed reproduction of Jerusalem which was an exact replica of Solomon's Temple on a Temple mount. Other projections on other walls showed a virtual Eden as far as 26 G could project it. Crystal clear streams larger than the Merced River were full of healthy trout and even sturgeon that had long been extinct. Realistic animals of all kinds roamed the meadows and would befriend anyone who touched them. The entire meadow appeared to be full of lush vegetation and groves of trees with loads of ripe fruit. In the center of the meadow was a huge Black Oak full of ripe acorns.

On one wall, which was the most popular, was depicted a virtual stairway to Heaven. Here people could step into the Hologram and have a virtual preview of the Rapture. Once on the stairway, they were transformed into angelic visages and whisked up into a mystic Heaven. Few seemed to notice that those who disappeared into the mist did not reappear when it vanished.

Sam had to begrudgingly admire how Satan had designed a virtual Paradise Theme Park, but he knew it was a real hell. He looked down to see people still getting out of the Tram and strained to see if one of them was Tiye. He wondered if she was captive or possessed. He wanted to believe she was held against her will. Even if that were true, how would he know if it was the real Tiye? Satan's virtual world was so real; who could tell the truth from lies anymore?

As he pondered those thoughts, a Holographic Projector crashed and what Sam saw made him shiver with dread.

The Tram morphed from a Luxury Transport to a line of *Güterwagen* railroad cattle cars hooked up to a German-made DRB class 52 steam locomotive once used by the *Deutsche Reichsbahn* for "relocation." The modern homes close by morphed into an endless line of brick buildings, of which 6 were two-stories, and 14 were single-story. It only lasted a moment before another projector came online, the Tram reappeared, and the buildings became modern again.

Most people were too busy having fun to notice, so few of them seemed concerned. Sam thought that maybe they deserved the hell that awaited them, but his heart would not let that thought linger.

All around the perimeter were huge megaBVR images of Malcolm dressed in his white robes with the golden girdles and his face was that of classical images of God. His honey-tongued speeches were said over melodious music and scenes of heavenly bliss.

Sam watched it fighting off puking before he decided to go down and get a closer look. He drove the Humvee hard on secret back trails to Lower Mariposa Grove and parked it nearby in thick Bull Thistle for cover. He got out of the Humvee and walked through the thistle. He got red blotches on his skin from the thistle spines but figured it was worth it. Finally, he stopped and ducked down behind the huge Sequoia known as the Fallen Monarch.

What he saw made him feel nauseous.

A huge swath of Giant Sequoias had been felled, and the land cleared to make room for the projected image of Solomon's Temple. A Tram was bringing in hundreds of people who were greeted by mega BVR Holograms of Prophets, who embraced each other as they got off the tram. At the entrance to the Temple, a visage of Malcolm dressed in High Priest's robes greeted each person, then let them pass inside.

Sam was not completely surprised to see John Pattos and Tiye helping Malcolm usher people into the Temple. He had to believe it was all holographic projections. He would not let himself believe Tiye or John Pattos would help Malcolm. He put his hand on the obsidian knife and wondered if it would cut out their chips without killing them.

As he watched, a man and his wife with their three small children tried to break free of the crowd and run. They were joined by a tall man in a Sikh's Turban, a man in a Franciscan monk's robe, people in Yarmulkes and traditional Nun's dress, along with Buddhist monks in saffron robes. Others dressed in street clothes clutched Bibles to their chests. All were incinerated by a fence of hidden lasers – lasers so powerful they cremated people without leaving a trace.

"My, God! Electronic Zyklon B!" Sam sighed.

"Yes, Sam." A voice interrupted his thoughts. He looked up to see John Pattos standing beside him. "Padre? You…"

"Hello, Sam."

"Okay, Malcolm. Nice Hologram."

"No, Sam. It's John. The hologram is the one in front of the Temple."

"Is there no end to the lies?"

"I am real, but just a messenger he believes you might listen to."

"Well go back and tell him he got that wrong."

Malcolm said to tell you he wants you to roam free. Except for the Temple. You will not be harmed if you do not interfere with any...."

"Interfere with what? A latter-day Holocaust?"

"Thousands may die but thousands will see paradise."

"That implant has your soul, John!"

"Sam, there is a colossal battle going on between celestial forces, and we need to stand aside and let it play out."

"Yes, except someone or something keeps getting me involved."

"And I began to weep bitterly because no one was found worthy to open the scroll." John mused.

"Okay, Padre. Screw the homilies. What's going on?"

"You are the worthy one, Sam?"

"Me? Of all people? That's insane."

"Do you know where the tree is that guards the book?"

"Tree? There are many here. What book?"

"The book of life."

"You got to be kidding me!"

"You are destined to open it."

"Look! I am the last guy any Deity would choose to do anything. I know the micro drones are listening. So, I hope your heard that, Malcolm!"

John looked around in fear. "You wear the sacred amulet that once adorned the Ahwahnechee Angels entrusted to guard the book," he whispered.

Sam started to touch the Golden Acorn. He hesitated, then turned to John, grabbed him by the neck and glared at him. "Ok! What are you up to messenger boy?"

John broke free and gathered his thoughts. "I...I don't understand."

"The Archangel Metatron guards the book of Life. No one else! So, what the hell is Malcolm up to?"

"You…are well versed in scripture for an atheist, Sam."

"Well, I know enough to know I'm no Enoch and Malcolm sent you to spy on me. So, get lost before I do something I will regret!" Sam balled his fists.

John backed off some. "You can defy, Malcolm, Sam. You cannot anger the spirts of Ahwahnee."

"Well, I don't intend to. Once I shut down Malcolm's projectors, I will turn my ears to the wind to see what the spirits have to say – if anything. Okay. Malcolm?"

"No, Sam. Do not provoke him. Please, for Tiye's sake."

"Ty?" Sam looked at the projected Tiye greeting people to enter the Temple. "Where is the real Ty?"

"She is to be his Queen."

"Of her own free will?"

"She really cares for you and is the only reason you're still alive."

Sam had to choke back anger and bitterness. His head was buzzing with conflicting thoughts, and he just wanted it all to go away. "What about your people? Can't you see he is killing them with that phony stairway to Heaven?"

"Do you not see the happiness on their faces as they are lifted into the Rapture?"

"Wake up, man! You can't believe…" Sam stopped when John held out the palm of his left hand which bore an implant scar. He nodded and felt some sympathy for John.

"Whatever you think of me, just think of Tiye before you do anything that might cause her harm."

"Cause her harm? Will she come as a Delilah, or a caring lover?"

"I tell you again; you live because of her."

Sam dared to believe she had sided with Malcolm to save his life. "Well, if I see her again, I will give her a big thank you hug!"

John looked scared and fell silent, then seemed to gather all the courage he had left. "Hurry, Sam! Come save us from the evil one!" John struggled for breath, gagged, and fell back in agony.

Sam saw his pain and knew the cause. "Let him alone, Malcolm! Let's you and I settle this all by ourselves!" Sam yelled at the wind and watched as John's pain seemed to ebb.

John caught his breath and looked past Sam.

Sam followed his eyes and turned to see three young children escape the selection line. They ran hard and thought they were free. There were smiles of relief on their young faces, just before they were instantly cremated by electronic Zyklon.

"My, God, Malcolm! Is there no limit to your depravity?" Sam screamed at a nearby mosquito drone.

John smiled, gave Sam a half nod, then looked very scared. "Listen!"

Sam perked his ear as he heard hoof beats and turned to see a Black Horse coming at him.

The Horseman was skeletal, with patches of skin hanging from bare bones, and he held a scale in one hand. In a dark mist that trailed behind him were a legion of skeletal men and women. The men were dressed in striped pajamas and the women in raggedy gray smocks. Before, they were huge bins of wheat and barley that were always just out of their desperate reach.

"Stop with the stupid Holograms, Malcolm! I don't buy it anymore!"

"A quart of wheat for a denarius and three quarts of barley for a denarius. Do not harm the oil and the wine." The Horseman said as the people held out empty hands begging for food. Wherever the Horseman rode, he left behind drought, barren earth, and famine. Then he rode up and stopped in front of Sam. "You have been measured and found wanting." The Horseman thundered as he rode past, then vanished as quickly as he had come.

Sam was a little unnerved for a moment then smirked. "Good production standards, Malcolm. But I'm still coming for you."

"I...don't think it...was a Hologram, Sam."

"Come on, John. It makes no sense."

"Belshazzar."

"Yeah, a Babylonian King. So what?"

"The handwriting on the wall."

"He freed Daniel but was killed anyway. What has that to do with me?"

John shook his head before he smiled. "I hope you find your calling before it…" John had to stop as the pain returned.

"Don't start that worthy business again. I…" Sam was interrupted by a mean looking Facista, who stopped ten yards away and unzipped his pants to pee. Sam eased up behind and decked the Facista before he got his pants unzipped, then he motioned for John to run toward the Humvee.

John hesitated, so Sam grabbed him by the scruff of the neck and pulled him along.

They were barely inside the Humvee when a bullet smashed into the windshield. Sam gunned the Humvee and headed across the meadow at full speed. He looked around to see five other Humvees coming at them from all sides. Bullets and Laser blasts peppered the Humvee like a hive of angry bees, yet not a single hit got through the thick armor. An RPG fired from a Humvee only a few yards away came just past Sam's window. It hit a Humvee that was coming directly at him and blew it up. Sam heaved a sigh of relief until the sound of a dozen rockets being fired brought him back to reality. He looked around to see all the rockets headed his way.

John bowed his head in prayer.

Sam saw the rockets headed straight at him. He touched the Golden Acorn and whispered a prayer. "O Great Chief! I am ready! Please grant me a spot in Elo'win." Seconds after he finished his prayer, the rockets passed directly over his Humvee turned in their course as if guided by an invisible hand. One by one, the rockets targeted all the Humvees chasing Sam, blowing them apart.

Sam drove his Humvee into a stand of Sequoias and stopped to catch his breath. He looked back across the meadow at the burning wrecks, turned to John, and sighed hard. "Maybe it's time to believe in something."

Malcolm had watched on a monitor and was fuming with rage. "Damn you, Michael! You don't have permission to do that!" He paused and shuddered. "Do you?"

Tiye, dressed in royal raiment and sitting on a golden throne, fought off a smile.

CHAPTER FOURTEEN

Now earth's blood poured from large open wounds at a million places East to West and North to South. It flowed in smoldering acid rivers that had the corrosive capability of one thousand times that of dimeric acid. Before every acid river, there was a phalanx of lightning bolts and, horrendously, reverberating thunder. The faithful stood fast and welcomed the thunder as Gabriel's horn. They saw the lightning as the fire of judgment. They sang songs of rejoicing as the river washed them away, as indifferently as it did the unfaithful who ran and tried to hide.

High, stratified clouds pulsated with brilliant rainbow colors all over the world. Their radiance surpassed the beauty of the brightest aurora borealis. People watched with awe and wonder until it began to drizzle acid rain that seared through everything it touched.

In the Great Plains, parched by drought, the rain was welcomed by thankful farmers who watched in horror as it burned the cornstalks to the ground. In the East, where a cooling shower would have once been a relief from the endless greenhouse heat, people scrambled for shelter only to find that the rain could burn away stone.

* * *

In the fire – ravaged Napa Valley, Hiram Holloway walked out into his small vineyard. All his helpers had long since deserted him. He was alone tending the few vines that had survived the plague of locusts. He was pleased to see the vines were plump with unseasonably ripe Cabernet grapes. Even though small, It was to be the best harvest he had, had in years.

Then acid rain began to fall.

Hiram worked with practiced grace at trimming the vines with the pruning shears. He felt the burning rain on his skin. It pelted him with hot beads of scalding water, but he ignored it and continued pruning. The hot rain soaked his clothes, and they began to smolder.

He would not be moved.

He believed in the End Times and the new earth that would bring forth a bountiful harvest blessed by God.

Hiram opened his heart and earnestly beseeched God to spare his vineyard. Moments later the rain ceased, and the earth seemed to move at his feet. He looked down to see it was no longer bleached and poor in nutrients but a rich dark loam. With a glad heart, he reached down to pick up a handful of his beloved soil. It was coal-black and as warm as beach sand.

Hiram had never seen soil like it. He almost cried as he rubbed it into his face. He was surprised to see it ease the hurt of the burning rain. He, lovingly, dug more of the strange soil. Reverently, he rubbed it all over his clothes and body. Where he was touched by the new earth, he was made whole.

All about him, the rain that had burned his vineyard ceased. Suddenly, he was in the eye of a storm that spread death and destruction all about – except for his small vineyard where he kneeled and honored the earth.

Hiram rejoiced as the plump grapes burst open and spewed his face with juice. The red juice trickled down his face and into the corner of his mouth. He started to spit it out. He hesitated as he felt on the tip of his tongue the finest vintage wine he had ever tasted.

*   *   *

117

In the Fiji Islands, the monsoons that once brought water and life now brought fire and destruction. The tribal elders gathered the people in the ceremonial "Long House" as their modern modular homes burned all around them.

The frightened islanders huddled in the natural grass hut and watched with mixed emotions as all about them the jungle burned. Every new thing the Elders had warned about burst into fire. Where something was made by man, it vanished in moments. Where something was taken, reverently from nature, it withstood the angry rain. The Elders' faces beamed with knowing smiles as the modern world evaporated and the old world withstood the fire.

An hour after the first acid rain had fallen, it stopped raining.

Slowly, the islanders moved from the "Long House" and knelt to pray in thanksgiving. All about them, the denuded jungle began sprouting buds. The once dingy sand now sparkled. The sea around them glowed as pure and clean as it had the day their ancestor had found it.

They sat close together and joined hands as they began to sing praises for the gifts of God.

CHAPTER FIFTEEN

Malcolm was still upset at Michaels's interference as he looked at the monitor and watched Sam drive the Humvee deep into a grove of trees. He turned the monitor off and looked at Tiye, who was being attended to by expert hairstylists and beauty experts.

"Can you make these people leave me alone?" Tiye tried to shoo the stylists away.

"No! They are only trying to enhance your beauty." Malcolm commanded.

"They can't make me something I am not."

"Oh? We will see." He drew close and looked at her with a wisp of melancholy. "You look so much like her. It's astonishing."

"I am not her, Malcolm!"

"Yes, you are – my Lillith!"

"Whom you believe was before Eve?"

"Yes. She, who was first and made of the clay of Eden, not the bones of man."

"Really? Not the way I heard it."

Malcolm's mood turned dark for a moment before he smiled again. "She would not serve a master, as would not I?"

The look on his face was so chilling Tiye had no reply.

Malcolm drew close and gave her a quick kiss. "Want to see Donavan and have some fun?"

"Yes…no…I have a headache."

Malcolm reeled backward for a moment, then chuckled.

"You know I don't allow those." Malcolm grabbed her arm to pull her along but was interrupted by Amon.

"Master, we have Sam on Secure Cam. He is headed to Mariposa grove as you predicted."

Malcolm thought it over a moment before he let go of Tiye and followed Amon to a Viewport.

Tiye sighed in relief.

They both watched on a monitor as Sam was still trying to recover from the Humvee attack when he saw a convoy of Military vehicles escorting a Presidential motorcade down the road toward the Lower Yosemite Falls. Trailing behind the motorcade and even more heavily guarded were a dozen armored vehicles containing ZZ Goons. "It's her. Damn! I knew it!" Sam cursed.

John followed his eyes. "Who?"

"See the Presidential seal on the limo?"

"The President here?"

"Yes."

"I…know why. I…" John flinched with pain.

Sam eyed John with suspicion. "I know why also, John." Sam spoke to the wind. "I know what you are up to, Malcolm."

John pushed through his pain to nod agreement.

"So, Malcolm! Stop shooting at me or I won't lead you to that tree?" Sam looked at the pain on John's face. "And stop with the pain impulses to my friend here."

John took a few moments to gather himself before he replied. "Thank you, Sam Please let's go to your tree and all will be well for everyone."

Sam looked at the scar on John's hand and wondered if God's power was greater than a micro-chip. "You still pray, John?"

John grimaced in pain and half-nodded.

"Well, I suggest you pray very hard because I suspect Malcolm now has the power, he needs to destroy the world."

John gave a frightened half-nod.

Sam revved the engine and drove fast. Just as he did, the sky turned dark with ultraviolet hues, and steel-jacketed hailstones began to pelt the Humvee. He looked at the radio on the dash that was undamaged. He turned it on, running the dial to the civil defense frequency.

"...*This is a repeat of an earlier broadcast. We are undergoing a national emergency because of natural occurrences. There is no act of war. We are not under attack. We are experiencing a natural phenomenon caused by severe sunspot activity. The refuge centers are safe. Please proceed to them...*"

Sam turned it off. "Sunspots? I wonder who he thinks believes all that?"

John's reply was to look at Sam with his face etched in agony. "No! He promised! He promised."

"What?"

"Look!"

Sam looked towards Cathedral Spires and watched as Reinhard X, a top einsatz gruppe Officer, was selecting who would go into Malcolm's temple or to the side into an area surrounded by an electronic force field. The einsatz gruppe ZZ Goons seemed to let only The Keepers go into the Temple. All others were packed into the fenced-off area. Anyone trying to go over the fence was vaporized.

"It seems you made a good bargain, John."

"He promised he would let all live."

"At least The Keepers will..."

"That was not my bargain, and he has killed many of my flock." They both looked at a digital display keeping count of the number of Keepers entering the Temple. After they were all in, it stopped at 143,999.

"That's quite a number he let live."

"It is not yet the sacred number. You must kill me now, Sam. Do not let me go back."

Sam was about to scoff when he saw the serious look in John's eyes. "You would make it an even..."

"Yes." John shivered with sadness. "And I looked, and I beheld the Lamb standing on Mount Zion and with Him one hundred and forty-four thousand, having His Father's name written on their fore-heads and His spirit in them."

"The Keepers of the Word specially chosen by God to go forth and bring mankind to repentance during the time of the tribulation." Sam added.

John was in so much pain he could barely nod.

Sam thought it over and looked at the sign reading 143,999. "So, he is one short."

John forced a painful nod.

"Why don't I take you to Pywiack. Its waters will cleanse you.

John was hit with intense pain and doubled over in agony. Sam pulled the obsidian knife from his clothing and held it up.

John's eyes pleaded for Sam to use it.

Sam hesitated just a moment before he took John's hand and cut the chip out.

John reeled back in relief praying for an easy death. It did not come. "Stop. Let me out, Sam.

"What? You are free now."

"No! Not until all are free."

Sam slowed the Humvee.

John opened the door and jumped out. "Go! Go, do what you have been chosen to do! As, will I!"

"You are the chosen one, not me."

"We have both been found wanting and need to fulfill our calling."

"I wish you luck my friend."

"Trust Tiye. She truly loves you! With God's grace and his Arch Angels we will prevail!" John turned and ran toward the Temple past the ZZ goons who stepped aside and let him enter.

Once John was inside the counter read: 144,000.

Then the steel door closed, and a darkness fell over the land.

Sam started to drive away but the Humvee would not start. He looked up to see a Demon Locust crash through the windshield and land beside him. The Demon Locust was as big as a hamster, and it had teeth sharp as razors. It tore at his right arm and began crawling toward his face. Blood was coming from bites on his arm when Sam was able to get the Obsidian knife and jab the Locust to death. He took a deep breath and blew it out hard. He was about to relax when he saw a cloud of locusts headed his way. The cloud was almost upon him when Sam got the Humvee started and roared off in the opposite direction. He grimaced as he drove hard. It was high noon, but the darkness blocked the sun. The sky formed huge crimson clouds that burst into a heavy rain of blood and giant frogs that smashed his windshield with slime that his wipers could not clean. He drove faster though he could not see where he was going. The loud thuds of flesh hitting his Humvee was deafening and he did not know how much longer he would make it. "Oh, Great Chief! I ask you for forgiveness and help. There is evil upon your sacred valley. Please grant me the wisdom and strength to stop it!"

Seconds later the Humvee came to a stop at a familiar spot.

Sam sighed in relief as he felt at home. He looked through a small spot in the dirty windshield and saw a huge Black Oak tree.

It beckoned to him.

CHAPTER SIXTEEN

Kate had mixed emotions about leaving Washington, but her Helicopter had left the White House lawn only moments before a caustic river had dissolved most of Pennsylvania Avenue and arrived at the wrought iron gates. As she had watched, the heavy wrought iron was dissolved in a split second. The East Lawn burst into flame, and the flames licked at the gallant old house – but it did not burn. The flames poured around the rose garden, but the flowers were not consumed. Kate had wondered at the scene as she looked at Miles.

Miles's look of rapture told her he could not have been happier. She did not share his "divine intervention" view as she considered the cold, hard work ahead. With a heavy heart, she booted up her laptop and had read quietly to herself from a list of people to be saved. Millions had applied and there was room for around one hundred and fifty thousand.

Kate was satisfied that she had set a good example by waiting until the last minute before abandoning the ship. She had tried a national TV address, but no transmissions were going out. Her closest communications advisors blamed "Atmospherics," but she smelled Malcolm Mabius. She was sure of it when it was his Private Jet and not Air Force One that flew her to Merced, where she was greeted by Amon and a dozen ZZ Goons.

Now she was in the back of her Presidential Limousine being driven to what her Military advisors had told her was the only safe place left on earth since Norad was in ashes. She knew Malcolm had them in his pocket. She welcomed confronting him and having it end one way or the other. For now, she had little choice but to go with them, hoping she would find a way to stop it all.

She held her finger off the computer mouse and looked at the icons and list of names. Now it was time to put an "X" for certain death or "Checkmark" for life.

Malcolm's was the first name on the approved list. She was told that she was bound by an agreement Hiram had signed to give space only to those who had made considerable contributions to his campaigns. She felt no obligation to honor that pledge and would pick people with needed skills and scientific backgrounds as those that should be saved. She deleted Malcolm's list and punched up one of her own.

There were extremely hard choices to be made.

Kate hesitated and thought it over as she looked at the names with a heavy heart: Harold Appelton, Agronomist; top-rated expert on crop management and production in depleted soil conditions. She moved her cursor and put a checkmark by Harold's name. Next was Tony Snow, Medical research specialist, specialty radiation sickness. Kate placed a checkmark by his name and continued to: Anne Spillman, research scientist; specialty chemical pesticides effect on ecology Kate placed another checkmark. Then read on: Early Santee, Nobel prize winner in literature.

Reluctantly, she moved the cursor to mark an "X" by Mr. Santee's name. A small tear formed in the corner of her eye as she remembered how much she loved his books.

Miles interrupted her thoughts. "The Russian Premier, the chairman, and all the heads of state that have survived have begged our permission to join us, Ma'am." Miles informed her politely.

"Which Russian Premiere? There were ten claiming that office at last count?" Kate wondered aloud.

"So, ignore the request?"

"Miles, do you like to play God?"

"Why no, ma'am. I would never presume, ever."

"Yes. I know your position. I don't like it either but look at what's happening. Malcolm said to limit the list to 12 people. So, who do we save? On anybody's list of who's important, I should be the first excluded," Kate insisted.

"No, Ma'am. You're the President," Miles snapped.

"I'm a token female who was appointed to a position because Hiram needed at least one female in his administration. My space should go to some brilliant scientist, artist, architect or deserving writer. In the new world, if there is to be, one will need the best we have. I was merely in a compromise pick because I had a military record and looked good on television."

"No, Ma'am. I can't let you get away with that. You were a distinguished soldier. You served in the most bitter fighting in the Golan Heights."

"That was somewhat personal."

"You are a hero of the Tel Megiddo Wars. Had you not stepped in after Hiram was killed, none of us would be alive. You brought us together when it was over, and it looked like we'd tear each other apart," Miles pleaded.

"Miles, you're the best aide a man…or woman…ever had. If my ego gets 'akilter, I know who to call. Now, I'm more in need of sage advice. I'm not God, Miles, and I don't want to make decisions about who should live and who should die," Kate sighed hard. "Please have the list sent to The Pope."

"Ma'am, last we heard, he was in the catacombs, and Rome is in ashes with no communication coming out." Miles cautioned.

Kate turned her face to the window of the Limo and pondered the information for a long moment. She had no way of knowing what sort of place Malcolm had prepared for himself. She watched as a portion of the rock at the base of The Cathedral Spires opened. She powered down her window and looked out.

The view was stunning.

Standing on a golden balcony, three stories above a street paved in gold, she could see Malcolm in Royal dress with a golden crown on his head.

Her soul felt an icy chill.

Sam looked at the big Black Oak and felt proud that it had grown into such a great tree. Looking upon it was pleasing to his soul. He started to get out of the Humvee and touch it. He grinned as he knew that was what Malcolm wanted him to do and decided to get as far away from it as possible and go to another tree. He drove away fast to withing a mile from the Lower Falls. He slowed to a stop as he saw the roadblock staffed by ZZ Robo Goons in *Schutzstaffel* uniforms.

They were Malcolm's *Geheime Staatspolizee* and were the evilest of the evil made up entirely of psychopaths, murderers, and rapists and led by a child molester Oskar Dirlewanger. All of them were Demons-in-training on parole from hell in the guise of einsatz gruppe ZZ Goons. Now that the Temple was at capacity, they were charged with the Cold-blooded execution of those not needed.

As Sam watched, they lured children into a Holographic petting zoo. The children screamed with delight as they entered it, and the animals gathered around them. The animals greeted the children with affection, and even the lions lying down by the lambs, allowed the innocent kids to hug them.

Sam knew it was a lie and that the ZZ Goons, disguised as benign Bo Peeps, would electronically cremate the children with lasers as soon as they were all inside the petting zoo. He took a deep breath and pushed the Humvee's accelerator to the floor.

The ZZ Goons heard the Humvee before they saw it. They turned and aimed their weapons as they signaled for Sam to stop.

Sam drove toward them at full speed.

The ZZ Goons were stunned for a moment before they kneeled and started firing their weapons point-blank at the Humvee. Their Laser Blasts should have torn through the Humvee's armor. Instead, they seemed to hit an invisible shield and bounce harmlessly off the Humvee's body.

Sam could believe what he saw but was thankful for it.

The ZZ Goons cursed a moment before they grabbed RPGs and knelt to fire them at Sam.

Sam was unsure that whoever or whatever was protecting him could stop the firepower of the new 26G66 RPGs. He flinched and tried to steer away from them as they fired. Moments later, his Humvee was shaken by explosions all around it. When the smoke cleared, Sam and the Humvee were not hurt. He looked to where the ZZ Goons had been and saw only a smoldering hole in the road. He shook a little as he stopped, got out of the Humvee, and walked to the petting zoo.

The children were a little stunned by the explosions and the disappearance of all the animals.

"Run as fast as you can to the forest and hide. Do not believe anything you see!" Sam barked.

The children hesitated.

"Now! Run now!" Sam yelled.

The children still hesitated.

Sam saw several unused RPGs in the bed of a nearby truck. He picked one up and aimed it at the ZZ Goons disguised as Bo Peeps. Now in demon form they came at Sam.

The children saw them for what they were and started walking, then broke into a run and disappeared into the nearby woods.

Sam fired the RPG and it exploded directly in front of the Demons with no effect. The Demons bared stiletto claws and huge fangs oozing drool as they came toward Sam. Sam grasped the necklace and whispered prayers. The Demons seemed fearful moments before and abyss opened and swallowed them whole.

Sam sighed in relief then looked up at a gnat drone. "Get ready, Malcolm. I am coming for you!"

"Damn him!" Malcolm cursed as he watched Sam on a monitor.

"That damn necklace!" Amon chortled.

"He never needed that; you fool! It's Michael and his tribe!"

"But it is forbidden for Michael to interfere."

Malcolm smiled a satisfied smile. "Then he is in rebellion."

"And he will join us in the pit!" Amon hoped.

Malcolm blew Amon down with the wind of his anger. "There will be no pit!"

Tiye glared at Malcolm. "You promised to spare the children!"

"They grow into vengeful adults soon enough." Malcolm snapped.

"I didn't bargain for this." Tiye started to remove her crown.

Malcolm turned and looked deep into Tiye's eyes. "Do you love this man?"

"I'm here with you, aren't I?"

"Enough to save him from a fool's death."

"Looks like he's doing ok."

Satan was not amused. "I can assure you it is only a matter of time until he is done."

"I had your promise."

"Conditioned on his going to the tree – not Pywiack."

"Oh? And you think I can persuade him to change his mind."

"Do you love him enough to try?"

"He will think I am a projection."

"Oh, I think he will know it's the real you."

"Even if he does, what makes you think he will listen to me? Malcolm grinned. "Because you are a woman, and this is Eden."

Tiye was not amused. "I am no Eve."

Malcolm thought it over and grinned. "No! At least not yet!" Before Tiye could reply, she found herself standing on Tioga Road. She looked up to see a Humvee with Sam behind the wheel coming her way. In a moment of whimsy, she stuck her thumb out for a ride.

Sam saw her, pushed the accelerator to the floor, and sped toward her. Tiye had to jump out of the way at the last moment to avoid being run over. She tumbled backward and rolled down an embankment.

Sam looked in the rear-view mirror. When he could no longer see her, he eased his foot off the accelerator and squealed the brakes to a stop. "What the hell?" He watched in the mirror until the dust settled, and he could see Tiye getting to her feet. His gut told him to drive on, but his heart made him turn around. Tiye was just getting to her feet and dusting herself off when Sam pulled up beside her. "Please! Enough with the holograms!"

"Believe me I am not one and wish I wasn't here!" Tiye growled.

Something in her tone and eyes made Sam sense she was real. "Why aren't you on your throne, Your majesty?"

Tiye's face seethed with anger as she turned to walk away.

Sam opened the passenger side door. "I have a brush if you want to dust yourself off?"

Tiye stopped and turned back. "You could have killed me, you idiot!"

"Nope! If I had wanted that, you would be dead."

Tiye thought it over and gave him a half nod.

"I'm headed to Pywiack to rid my soul of evil. Want to join me?"

Tiye glared at him, then mellowed a little before she looked scared then her eyes misted with sadness.

Sam looked at the sadness on her face and saw kindness in her eyes more real than any megaBVR hologram, so he decided to play it out. "Get in. This might be fun."

Tiye hesitated then got in.

"So, Malcolm, what adventures do you have in store for me Now?"

Tiye looked hurt a moment then replied. "I think I am supposed to convince you to give up and be a good boy."

"No can do!"

"What you decide will affect the lives of thousands, Sam."

Her voice sounded so real and there was an aura of the real Tiye around her. Besides, he wanted to believe it was her. "Weren't you supposed to be his queen?"

"Not for me. Too much work to stay queen-like." "Won't you miss, Donavan?" Sam smirked.

Tiye turned and looked out the window and waited for a time before replying. "What would you believe?'

Sam took her face in his hands and gave her a long, deep kiss. When he broke it, he sensed she was real but did not let down his guard completely. "The new projections, can fake a kiss?"

"We are still working on that."

"OK, did he send you, or is this your idea?"

"Maybe a little of both?"

"So, what message do you have for me from Lucifer?"

"That you were right."

"Oh?"

"He is…Satan,"

"He finally admitted it?"

"I saw what he did to the children."

Sam shuddered in remembrance. "Yes…yes…can you not make him stop that?"

"Would you believe I tried?"

"And?"

"The Holocaust was one of his favorite times. He watches reruns every night."

Sam stopped the Humvee and gripped the steering wheel hard. "What the hell are you up to, and don't lie. I have had enough of that, and it's hard not to strangle that pretty neck!"

"He still holds John and his Keepers captive. If I have your promise not to interfere in his plans, he will not harm them or any more children."

"Not harm them. Have you seen the electronic Zyklon in action?"

"That is ended. All he requires now is The Keepers to attend. worship service twice a day. They are fed well and have lavish quarters."

Sam gave her a steady gaze. "What about me scares him so much he sends you and John and giant frogs and huge locusts to confront me?"

"His demons like to have their fun. He made sure you weren't harmed."

Sam looked at her with mixed emotions of love and hate. At times, when their eyes met, he could see love lost, then his mind would caution him, and he had to turn away. He touched the Golden Acorn and smiled. "Yes, he knows Tenaya is protecting me."

"No, he thinks it's Michael, the Archangel."

"What?"

"Seems they are old enemies."

"Biblically true and if real in our time, something we should stay the hell out of."

"I wish that were possible."

"In any case, tell me the real reason he sent you."

"Would you believe, I don't really know."

"Nope."

"He keeps talking about a Tree and a Book you might lead him to."

"And if there is such a tree and book, what if I do lead him to them?"

"Honestly, I don't know."

"Yeah! I think Omar Khayyam was right. Oh, what an endless game he plays!"

"Then one by one, back in the closet he lays?"

Sam and Tiye share quiet agreement.

"I don't like being a pawn in anyone's game! I wish they would all leave me alone. It's ridiculous to think I would be a divine messenger boy when I don't believe in God!" Sam insisted.

"Maybe, he believes in you."

"Well, am I done with it. You and Malcolm and all the rest can have your little haven and celestial games. Just leave me alone at Pywiack."

"Perhaps if you go to your tree, he will allow that for you."

Sam held the Golden Acorn with reverence. "He can't harm me. It's not Michel. It's Tenaya and Ahwahnechee angels. They will not let Malcolm prevail. Hear that, Malcolm?"

Tiye shook her head a little scared. "Well, I have said my piece. I hope you are right, but I would not count on that trinket helping."

"That's why you came?"

"What?"

"To take it away." Sam held the Golden Acorn tight.

"No, Sam. I am here to urge you to lead him to the tree and he will let you go to Pywiack." Tiye started to open the door. "Just do it and get it over with!"

Sam grimaced and looked apologetic. "I would love to if I knew what the hell he was talking out."

"I thought you said…"

"I said what I thought he wanted to hear. You pick a tree! OK?"

Tiye looked doubtful then chuckled. She opened the door and started to exit. "Take care of yourself, Sam."

"Come to Pywiack with me. The spirits in the water will cleanse you from his evil."

Tears formed in Tiye's eyes, and she looked at him with love. "Don't you know I am his once and future queen?"

Sam was about to reply when Tiye got out and ran away.

He started to go after her but hesitated knowing that was what Malcolm wanted and he was determined never to do what Malcolm wanted again.

That is what his head told him.

His heart insisted he follow and make sure she was ok.

Kate was bored in splendid isolation. Her room was a huge suite with magnificent flower arrangements and a buffet table always full of delicious food. She was not hungry, and she sighed hard.

Miles worried about her. "You want to talk?"

"Yes. I think we exactly know what he wants." Kate replied. Miles held the "football" close to his chest smiled as he watched the deep regret in her eyes and wondered how much she hurt inside. "I believe it is as you suspect."

"The codes?" Kate insisted.

Miles nodded.

Kate looked at her right arm and a small pink dot on it. "Any chance he can access the implant?"

"No, Ma'am!"

"Only my touch will work. If I am dead, he cannot access them, right?"

Miles nodded a slow, reluctant nod. "Please don't even suggest that."

"One life to save many?" Kate pulled an earring from her ear and opened it to reveal a small pill. She closed it and smiled.

Miles looked horrified.

"Only as a last resort, Miles." Kate moved to the buffet table. "Now, what's for dinner? I am starved."

Miles moved to the buffet table and uncovered a dish of sautéed mushrooms and small pieces of tofu. "These look good."

"Mushrooms? Very appropriate considering how they're grown," she smiled.

"Ma'am?"

"Kept in the dark and fed…"

"I know, Ma'am!"

"Stop with the Ma'am, my dear friend. All the protocol is over. Now sit down and join me and let's talk about this brave new world that Mr. Huxley isn't here to help us with," Kate forced a smile.

Miles sat down and nibbled at the small plate of mushrooms. They ate quietly, suppressing any hint of the fear each felt.

Tiye had not gone far when she stopped and waited for a helicopter from Malcolm to come pick her up. She was close to Pywiack Dome, and it was a good spot for one to land. All she saw was an empty sky and quiet, until she heard Sam's Humvee approach.

Sam drove hard until he approached Pywiack Dome. He was almost blinded by the bright sun that glistened dazzling white on the granite face of Pywiack Dome polished by countless ancient glaciers. The bright light caused him to come to a stop to regain his bearings. When his sight returned, he was amazed to see he had stopped by a Great Black Oak that was shrouded by a dark shadow. He was more surprised to see Tiye standing by it. He pulled to a stop, got out of the Humvee, and approached her. "You didn't get far."

"Guess I missed my ride."

They fell quiet and both looked at the huge Black Oak tree. "I see you found a tree." Sam mocked.

"Oh? Is it *the* tree?" "Could be. You tell me."

"I think it is. You have won."

Tiye looked saw the mischievous look in Sam's eyes and decided to play along.

"So, I was to lead him to a Tree? Here it is, Malcolm." Sam's voice echoed across the valley.

There was no reply.

Sam paused and looked at the magnificent Great Black Oak. It was a splendid Black Oak that stood alone among granite slabs where no tree had ever grown. Around it was hundreds of acorns that seemed to shine golden in the midday sun. The bright sun reflected off Pywiack Dome, yet the tree was in shadow.

"I don't remember seeing this tree here before." Tiye looked at the tree, then back at Sam. "Maybe you have fulfilled your quest."

Sam touched the tree with reverence, then stood back. "Yes. It is a miracle tree. No trees are supposed to grow here in the upper basin. It's all granite domes." He picked up an acorn and held it with reverence. "Now may I go to Pywiack in peace?" Sam appealed to the wind.

He expected a holographic reply from Malcolm. None came. "What now?" He looked to Tiye for an answer.

"I'm just waiting on my ride." Tiye shrugged.

Sam took her hands in his. "Come to Pywiack with me."

Tiye looked at him with love, her eyes tinged with sadness. "I see that you are left in peace there."

Before Sam could reply, hey were engulfed in a heavy Tule Fog. The Tule Fog was so dense she could not see Sam and he could not see her.

Sam peered into the Tule Fog and heard drumbeats. As he listened, it cleared enough so that he could see Ghost dancers around a nearby fire. He watched as they tossed wormwood into a fire and chanted ancient songs as they danced. Sam felt someone put a bearskin coat around his shoulders. He turned to see Tenaya standing before him. "Is this the place? Tell me what to do, and I will do it! O Great Chief!" Sam asked as he began to kneel.

"Savage is upon Ahwahnee again! This time, Uzumaiti must eat!" Tenaya responded.

"Yes! I am here to do your will."

"Listen! None can hear in this sacred fog, but you."

"I hear and obey. Now tell me what…"

"Evil eyes are upon you. This was to deceive the great deceiver."

"I…I really want to understand?"

"You cannot go to Pywiack until the sacred land is free of the evil one."

"Yes. Okay. But how? What do I do?"

"You will find what you seek in the shadow of Tesa'ak!"

"Please! What am I looking for?"

"The Tree was once laden with sweet fruits. It protects The Book of Life and must not be touched any but the worthy one."

"How will I know this tree?"

"When you know yourself, you will know all else."

"I don't understand?"

"We were set at the gate in the beginning. You are the last Ahwahnechee guardian. You must not let the unworthy one touch the book."

"I? Me? I am Ahwahnechee?" Sam hoped with a burst of pride."

"The Great Spirit has chosen; it is for us only to obey!"

"I...I will do what you ask, Great Chief. Just guide my way."

"Only the lamb may touch the book. Stand tall before the evil winds and gird yourself with the spirits. You have thrown off the silk coats of shame! Now do honor to your people!" Tenaya thundered then disappeared in the mist.

Sam was stunned by the encounter. The smell of burned worm-wood was still in the air, and he knew it was no hologram.

Yet his mission was no clearer than it had been before. He did know that there was no turning back. His native soul would not allow it now. He was almost crushed by a feeling of Deja vu – Deja vu for the loss of kind people in a savage time. Then he felt a surge of strength even more powerful than The Black Dog. Strength tempered with cunning. It was the most wonderful sense of belonging he had ever felt.

"I am Ahwahnechee!" Sam beamed.

For a long time after the fog had lifted, he smiled with pride until Tiye broke into his thoughts.

"Sam? I was worried. I couldn't see anything through the fog."

"Did you hear the drums?"

Tiye shook her head.

"Then he didn't hear either." Sam looked at a mosquito drone.

"Hear what?"

"Never mind. I have led Malcolm to the tree so let's just part now as friends. I am sure your ride will be along soon."

Tiye looked at him and his eyes were golden brown and seemed to shine with a peaceful countenance. "You look and sound different. I think you have found your calling."

"I cannot take you with me."

"So, this is the tree he wants?"

Sam saw a gnat drone nearby. "Yes, Malcolm. Here it is. Now you can have the world. Just leave Pywiack to me."

Tiye looked at him with pleading eyes and he knew she wanted to go there with him. "I envy you, Sam."

"You love it as much as I?"

Tiye nodded.

Sam looked at her with love. "You will always be welcome there."

"I wish that with all my heart. But I have promises to keep."

"John and his flock?"

Tiye nodded, then turned to walk away.

Sam touched her shoulder and held her back. "The book of life?"

"Yes?"

"What do you know about it?"

"*Lshana tova tikatevu!*"

"What?"

"May you be inscribed and sealed in the Book of Life for a good year. On Rosh Hashanah, the blowing of the ram's horn means it's time to open the book of life and examine whether we have been naughty or nice. Then you spend the next ten days reflecting and remembering. After fasting on Yom Kippur, The Shofar blows, you close the book, hopefully with your name still in it."

"...hopefully..." "...hopefully..."

"What does it look like?"

"No one knows, Sam. God wrote it even before creation." "If this was Eden, it was here at the beginning. Yeah! Isn't it the book to be opened on Judgement Day by the worthy one?"

"Only one of the lineages of David can do that."

"Lineage of David like you?"

"Oh, no? Besides, it couldn't be here."

"Why not?"

"No serious biblical scholar puts Eden anywhere near here."

"I know. They say Mesopotamia?"

"It's anybody's guess."

Sam looked at the Black Oak tree nearby. "Well, here it is. You guys have fun." Sam looked past her and saw Amon and Oskar in a Humvee. "Looks like you ride is on the way."

"Be safe at Pywiack, Sam?"

"Well, not sure where I am going or what exactly I am going to do, but I think I'd better listen to the winds." Sam looked at her and she saw doubt but determination in his eyes before she followed them to see him looking at Amon and Oskar in a Humvee headed her way.

"Do what you are called to do, Sam. I will give try to get you the time." Tiye gave him a quick kiss, then turned and moved toward Amon's Humvee.

Sam watched as Oskar opened the door for her to get in.

Tiye looked back for a moment before she got into the vehicle with them. There was an honest aura to her face – he ached to believe.

"I hope you will be happy, Queen, Lil!" Sam yelled at her. There was no reply as once she was inside the Humvee, Amon gunned the Humvee's engine and headed straight for Sam at full speed.

Tiye fumed at Amon. "No! No! You promised to leave him alone and let John go if he led you to the tree."

Amon slapped her down with a backhand. "You pitiful woman! You never learn!"

Tiye wiped the blood from her lip. "Why? I have done as Malcolm wanted?"

"Then his usefulness is at an end!" Oskar snarled before he and Amon chuckled, and for a moment, showed their hideous Demon selves.

"Then you mean to kill him? No! Not my deal!" Tiye tried to open her door. It was tightly locked. She looked up to see Sam jump aside just as Amon drove within inches of him.

Sam fell hard as Amon began to turn the Humvee around to go at Sam again. He struggled to his feet and was barely inside his Humvee when Amon roared by with a near miss.

Sam gritted his teeth and gunned his Humvee hard toward them. He was ready to crash head-on if need be.

Amon's Humvee had forward fired Maximum Range: M134 GAU-17 "Vulcan" six barreled cannons. He pressed the firing button and loosed 6000 rounds toward Sam's Humvee."

"That's not going to do you any good. He is protected." Tiye had to stop as bullets riddled Sam's Humvee and blew out both front tires.

Sam lost control, and his vehicle narrowly missed a huge granite rock but crashed into a smaller one. The airbag deployed and knocked Sam woozy. He did not remember getting out or where he was until he looked up at Amon's ginning face.

"You shoulda' fetched your K-9 friend?" Amon sneered.

Sam tried to rise but was too dizzy. He whispered a prayer to Tenaya for help. There was no answer, and he felt even weaker.

"Praying for your digger Indian chief to help?" Amon needled.

Sam swung at Amon and missed.

"Trying to defend the honor of a woman who betrayed you, Sam?" Amon motioned for Oskar to bring Tiye to his side.

Tiye did not seem to mind.

"Has an ugly ogre like you ever had a woman who wasn't forced to like you?" Sam sneered.

Amon looked upset a moment before he took Tiye's right hand and held it out. "See, Sam. No implant. She comes with us of her own free will."

Sam had no reply as he and Tiye exchanged forced glances.

"Queen Lil, want to say any last goodbyes?" Oskar grunted.

Tiye had to respond with a reluctant shake of her head. She looked at Sam with eyes that seemed to call for help before they faded in pain.

"Is Malcolm so desperate for a queen, he has to enslave one?" Sam growled. He suspected, despite no implant, she was under

Malcolm's control. It was too painful to believe otherwise. "Tell your Master to let her go. I have led you to the tree." Sam offered.

Amon motioned for Oskar and him to stand aside, then looked at Tiye "You are free to go to him?"

Tiye started to move toward Sam, stopped and grimaced then backed away.

"See, Sam. She is Lillith and will be his Queen." Oskar said as he opened the back door of the Humvee and motioned for Tiye to get in.

Tiye started to get in, stopped clenched her fists in pain, turned and looked at Sam.

"Whatever he promised. Tiye he will not do. He is the Prince of Liars. Come with me to Pywiack and we will be safe from his power." Sam pleaded.

Tiye thought it over and started to move toward Sam.

Oskar grabbed her arms and pulled her down to the ground.

Amon kicked her in the side, drew his gun and aimed at her.

Tiye grimaced in pain and shoved Oskar aside before she took off running in the direction of Half Dome.

Amon and Oskar stared at each other wondering how to react, then both pulled guns and aimed to fire at her.

"Leave her alone, you creeps!" Sam yelled and moved toward them. Sam called for The Black Dog. It was slow to awake.

Amon and Oskar jumped into the Humvee.

Oskar saw Amon triggering the cannons. "These mortals are so tiresome. Let's blow them both away, no matter what the Master says!"

Oskar started to fire but was interrupted by the cannons locking up and a hologram of an angry Malcolm appearing.

"Do not fire on them!" Malcolm ordered.

"You sure, Master? He has led us to the tree."

"You idiot! That was not the tree!"

"What should we do?"

"You? You will do nothing but descend to the Harpies!" Malcolm boomed.

Amon and Oskar cowered in fear before they morphed back to minor Demons and were sent spiraling into a portal, through the gates of hell into a nest full of Harpies. They both gasped in horror as Harpies encircled them with wings spread and sharp beaks that gnawed at them with stiletto teeth.

Moments later, Eric Koch and Ilse Koch appeared. Each with visible noose marks on their necks. Eric and Ilse were two of Malcolm's favorite Demons and, at times, more satanic than he.

Eric sat in the driver's seat and Ilse beside him in the passenger seat.

Ilse glared at Eric.

Eric hesitated a moment, then let her move to the driver's side.

"What would you have us do, Master?" They said in unison. "Bring me my Queen unharmed."

"Destroy the man?" "No!"

"He is defying you, Master!"

"Do as you are told!" Malcolm clicked off.

Moments later, Ilse turned the Humvee away from Sam to pursue Tiye.

Sam saw The Humvee bearing down on Tiye at full speed.

It was close on her when she tripped and fell.

Ilse was barely able to stop the Humvee in time to avoid running over Tiye.

Eric got out of the Humvee, grabbed Tiye by the arm and tried to pull her into the Humvee.

Tiye scratched at his eyes. Eric punched her and Tiye fell to the ground. As she lay there Eric cursed at her wiping a trace of blood off his cheek.

The Black Dog whimpered with indecision, until Eric kicked Tiye hard in her left side. On seeing that, The Black Dog was at full killing force as he loped toward Eric.

Eric looked up to see The Black Dog coming and motioned Ilse to shoot.

Ilse shook her head vigorously. "No! The Master forbids."

Eric nodded agreement, picked Tiye up, and threw her in the back of the Humvee. He was barely inside himself when Ilse drove off at full speed.

The Black Dog was full out when it leaped and landed on top of the Humvee with a loud thud. They were close to Half Dome's edge when Ilse turned the steering wheel sharply. The Humvee spun so hard that The Black Dog was thrown off the roof, the back door opened, and Tiye rolled out. She rolled within inches of going over the cliff.

She sighed in relief until she saw The Black Dog coming at her.

The Black Dog loped up to Tiye, paused, and growled. Tiye looked on in fear. "No, Sam. Seek your *yetzer ha'tov! Tikkun olam!*"

The Black Dog snarled and bared its teeth.

Tiye shook her head, and tears formed in her eyes as The Black Dog snarled at her and bared fangs. He was rabid with anger. His fangs were inches from her throat.

"I love you, Sam. No matter what you see or hear, believe only that! You must save Ahwahnee and save the world!"

The Black Dog was almost full out as the word "Ahwahnee" echoed in its ears. For an instant, he was Sam, and his eyes met hers in a kind of remembrance that caused The Black Dog to back off.

"No! No!" Tiye yelled as she saw Eric about to plunge an obsidian knife into The Black Dog.

Before The Black Dog could react, Eric drove the obsidian knife into The Black Dog's back. The Black Dog yelped in pain, leaped off Tesa'ak and tumbled to the valley floor.

"Oskar told me that would work." Eric was pleased with himself.

Malcolm was not. He had a legion of Harpies appear and drag Eric to hell.

Ilse watched and took her hands off the gun trigger.

Tiye got to her feet and looked down at the valley floor. She saw no trace of Sam or The Black Dog. "Oh. God no! Malcolm you will have nothing from me for doing this!"

Malcolm appeared beside Tiye in a Holocast. "They know the penalty for disobeying me?"

Tiye looked down at the valley floor empty of anyone. "I have done all you asked. Is John free now?"

"I don't think you have helped at all."

"All I did was promise to try. What Sam does is not my problem."

"Oh, yes, it is."

"I knew you would not keep your, promise."

"I am not finished yet."

"Well, I am."

"You are defying me?"

Tiye began to back away. She watched as Malcolm sniffed the air "Bad air, Malcolm?"

"Do you not smell angel dust and know what forces are arrayed against me?'

Tiye sniffed the air. "Smells like roasted acorns and burned wormwood to me."

Malcolm's face contorted in anger, then he had to smile and nod.

"Then you know there is much more to do."

"I don't feel bound by our deal any longer. Can I take a walk?"

"You are free to go. But where?"

"I feel dirty."

"You have splendid baths here at the sanctuary."

"For the flesh."

"Yes, and handmaidens to dry you off, perfume and pamper you."

"I need to go to Pywiack to cleanse my soul – saying, of course, that I still, have it?"

Malcolm's Hologram flashed red hot then cooled and he smiled. "You will come running back when the fires consume all but my Temple."

Tiye did not reply but moved away from the Holocast as fast as she could.

"I will get her, Master. I will not fail you." Ilse pleaded. "No!"

"She will get away."

"You want to join, Eric?'

"No. Master. I just want to do your will."

"You have. "Malcolm smiled. "It is all going as planned."

Malcolm was pleased with himself until he sniffed the air and smelled Angel Dust. "No! Not now. But soon! Hear that, Michael? Soon!"

CHAPTER SEVENTEEN

The earth was now at its peak of violent activity. Except for the Himalayas, a small part of New Mexico, and Yosemite, the earth was throwing back every effluent ever poured into its tissue and pouring it back more robust, wider, deeper, and meaner. There was no night or day but an orange, black-orange twilight that covered the face of the land. The oceans were covered with a layer of gray silt from the ash and smoke of a million volcanoes. Volcanoes erupted with terrible resounding booms that dwarfed Hydrogen bomb sounds.

The electric storms that accompanied the volcanoes walked across the face of the earth and blew away what they did not burn. The continental drift in places was so severe that land masses crashed into each other, breaking into pieces like good china being rammed against bad peanut brittle. Burning, corrosive, acid rain fell behind the electric storm, and there was no relief for anyone still left on the surface.

Sam had no sensation of falling.

Instead, there was the wonderful sense of relief that soon he would shed his flesh and know, at last, if there exists any trace of a spirit within his body. In any case, he would be dead, and so would The Black Dog.

Peace without pain was so wonderful to contemplate.

It seemed he had fallen for eternity when he found himself in Ahwahnechee buckskin clothing, standing before Chief Tenaya, who was clothed in Ahwahnechee Ceremonial dress.

"Welcome to Elo'win!" Tenaya said as he offered Sam a bowl of acorn mush in a willow basket.

"Oh, thank you Great Chief." Sam sighed in relief. He took the bowl and began to eat. The taste was so bitter he spit it out.

Seconds later he could not catch his breath and knew he was drowning.

Tiye crawled into a stand of Bull Thistle and crouched down when she heard propellers. She looked up to see a Helicopter heading her way with Ilse in the pilot's seat of a Modified Super-Apache SAH 66 attack Helicopter. At her side, as a copilot, was Oskar. Malcolm had recalled Oskar from Harpie hell and ordered them to track Tiye knowing she would lead him to Sam. Both had seen what had happened to Eric, so they were determined to fulfill this mission. They both bore scars from Harpy bites. Each pondered if they had a chance for revenge if they would have the nerve to take it.

Tiye did not know which way to run. The thistles tore at her clothes and skin, but she felt safe among them until she heard the chopper now directly overhead. Tiye looked up to see Ilse's face. There was still some distance between them, but the look of evil on Ilse's face looking his way gave her a chill.

"That's her in those bushes," Oskar said before Malcolm's voice cracked on the radio.

"You fools! I said track her from a distance. Now she knows you are there."

Oskar and Ilse glared at each other.

"Ilse was always a disobedient one, Master."

"It's Oskar's fault…"

"Shut up. Both of you. Just bring her to me!" Malcolm ordered then signed off.

Tiye could see through a break in the Bull Thistle that the chopper was landing in a small clearing – only thirty yards away. She watched as Oskar got out of it and headed her way. Then she crawled forward out of the thistle, ripping her clothes more and experiencing painful cuts to her skin. She got to her feet and looked around, trying to see the best way to run.

"Don't run. Malcolm just wants to talk." Oskar yelled. Tiye took off running.

In the Chopper, Ilse pulled the trigger on the Gatling guns, and bullets smacked into the ground all around Tiye, causing her to freeze in place. As she looked back, Tiye saw Oskar's face. His face was pitted and scarred, and his eyes glistened with evil lust. Lust more intense than that of Amon, whose mere touch made her retch.

Death was much more appealing.

Tiye looked toward the cliff. She took a deep breath and blew it out hard. Then she ran as fast as she could toward the cliff's edge.

Oskar was right on her heels as she reached the edge.

Tiye stopped and looked down. It was inviting to leap and escape all responsibility. After all, what did she really owe John and The Keepers. She started to ease forward and leap, but Oskar pulled her back and held her tight.

Tiye kicked and bit at him until he slugged her, and she went limp.

Oskar gathered his breath, then carried her to the Chopper and threw her inside, "Damnation! I think we should kill her now."

"What did you say? "Malcolm's voice crackled on a speaker.

Oskar stopped when a hologram of Eric being eaten by a dozen Harpies appeared. "Forgive me. I was just thinking…"

"Stop thinking. Just bring her to me." Malcolm commanded surrounded by Harpies, their serpents' teeth dripping with the juice of anticipation.

The sight of the Harpies sent shivers down Oskar's spine. "No, Master. We will not fail again."

Ilse enjoyed Oskar's pain then spoke up. "We will find Sam without her, Master."

"Sam is where I want him to be. Do not approach him until I say so!"

"Please tell us where so we may avoid him."

"Stay away from the river."

"Yes, Master. Which river?" Ilse asked before she could stop herself.

Oskar eyed Ilse with hate. "The stupid woman asked, Master. Not I."

"Avoid all rivers or I will make a new circle of hell just for you beyond any you can imagine – idiots!"

Ilse and Oskar slapped at each other and growled, then flew off trembling with fear.

Sam awoke in the Merced River.

It was at flood stage, and it carried him along so fast he could not get his bearings. The water was near freezing and full of tons of construction debris and fallen trees that swirled about him. A heavy tree limb hit him with a glancing blow and sent him under. He struggled to get back to the surface, but the speed of the water kept pulling him there. He gasped for air and tumbled over and over, not knowing which way was up.

"O Great Chief! Please! Take me to Elo'win now!" Sam mumbled a silent prayer. His answer was the sound of an I-Beam and broken limb of a Giant Sequoia banging against each other. The log hit him squarely in the back and pushed him to the surface. He broke the surface of the water, gasping for breath. Moments later, he was caught up in a whirlpool that started taking him down again. He struggled at first but then felt a strange sensation of peace.

Maybe here, at last, was how he was to die. He relaxed and waited for the peace of oblivion.

Tiye was curled up in the cargo space of the Chopper. She turned to look up at Oskar's hideous face. She retched, and he did not like it.

"You think you are too good for someone like me?" Oskar got up from the co-pilot's seat and eased so close to Tiye she could smell his wretched breath.

Tiye turned away without replying.

Oskar grabbed her face in his hands and turned her back. "I used to have a dozen Jewish Princesses like you before lunch! How about a little kiss?" Oskar grinned then puckered to kiss her.

Tiye forced a smile. "Sure!" Tiye pulled his head toward hers and breathed hot air into his left ear.

"Okay, Baby! Yeah! That's better," Oskar reached down to unzip his pants. Before, he was half unzipped. Tiye shoved his face aside, bit down on his left ear, and took a chunk out of it.

Oskar cried out in pain as he released her. He fell back against Ilse causing her to fall against the steering Yoke and the Chopper began to spin out of control.

"You stupid woman! Get control now!" Oskar yelled at Ilse as he fell against a wall.

"Don't call me stupid, you *shweinhund*!" Ilse tumbled to the floor as the Chopper went way off course.

Tiye spat out Oskar's ear and looked down to see she was above the river. It was a thirty-foot fall, and if the fall didn't kill her, she might drown. She looked up to see blood oozing from Oskar's ear and unbridled rage on his face. It was clear no orders from Malcolm would stop him now. She closed her eyes and remembered an old prayer her Grandfather had taught her. "O, God! Thrice 50 times will I lift my hands unto thee. Be it unto me as it pleaseth thee, and thy holy Ministers. I require nothing but thee, and through thee, and for thy honor and glory. I hope you shall be satisfied and shall not die until thou gather the clouds together and judge all things and when in a moment I shall be changed and dwell with thee forever." Tiye prayed. Then she leaped out of the chopper and fell toward the river.

Sam was drowning and he thought he heard foot drums, split-stick clappers, and bone whistles. As he felt himself descending into the deep, he saw a vision of Tenaya in ceremonial dress surrounded by dancing warriors. As the Ahwahnechee danced, the spirits of the dead arose and began pointing fingers at Sam, then at Poo-see-na-chuck-ka.

"I am sorry. I have failed you, Great Chief. For this I do not deserve a place in Elo'win" Sam struggled for breath. He touched the Golden Acorn and saw a vision of Major Savage, holding the hand of a lovely Indian Maiden. They looked at Sam in a small bed and smiled.

"Which world shall we give him?" Major Savage asked.

"The one with the most love." The Maiden replied.

"I am not loved by either world!" Sam cried out with his last breath.

Tiye had to struggle to get her breath. Not only was the water cold, but it was moving fast and full of debris. She was hit several times by small logs and barely avoided some huge ones. Finally, she was able to hold onto a Black Oak Tree branch and catch her breath. She looked up to see The chopper some distance away, so she kept her head down as much as possible. Each time she popped her head up, she could hear the angry whine of machinery butchering Giant Sequoias. Whatever tree he was after, was not in Mariposa Grove – if he was after a tree at all. She recoiled at the thought of returning to Malcolm and having to endure his ego-drenched presence while he tortured The Keepers and planned to destroy the world. She knew she was the only one who could stop him. To do that she had to be in his control room. That meant as much as she hated it, she would have to endure Oskar and whatever Malcolm had in store, but she had to return to him, and hope Sam would just stay out of the way.

With a heavy heart, she eased her way from log to log until she was close enough to the shore to try to pull herself out of the river. She was almost there when a log cracked her in the back of her head and sent her down. She struggled for the surface but was too weak to swim up. She began to drown and started to recite old prayers. Moments later, A surge of water lifted, and she was thrown onto the riverbank where she lay still and looked to the heavens with a prayer of thanksgiving.

Sam gasped for breath as some unseen hand propelled him to the surface. Once there, he found himself caught in a whirlpool that took him up fast and threw him on the riverbank. He landed hard and lay still. As he lay there his thoughts flashed back to the vision. He was a little pleased by it. He wanted to believe that if, by no one else, he was loved by those who gave him life. That thought made the Black Dog growl – and he knew love was the way to make it lie down forever. Now he would give his all to save Ahwahnee and then he and his mother would be granted a place in Elo'win.

Sam's life force was now strong, but his lungs were drowning. He gasped for breath. His lungs struggled to inhale a last ounce of air. He fought them to fill with air. There was some pain, but he expected that would pass soon.

He felt the creeping coldness of death.

Then he felt the warmth of familiar lips on his.

It was a welcome kiss and forced the breath of life back into his body. He began to cough hard. As he coughed out death and breathed in life, he opened his eyes to behold Tiye kneeling beside him. She was about to push down on his chest. He looked at her with love, then concern. "No! Tiye?"

"You're welcome."

Sam sat up and looked confused. "How? What are you…"

"Whoa? That's the thanks I get?"

"How? What?"

"Just trying to survive…like you."

Sam eyed her with suspicion. "I thought you were his darling Queen!"

Tiye glared at him, then looked dead serious. "If I had known my surviving would upset you so much, I would have let them kill me."

Sam looked at her, and his ire cooled. He had to let out a sardonic laugh at it all.

Tiye did not find him amusing.

"I'm sorry. I'm…I'm all messed up." Sam smiled.

"More than usual?"

"No! Better, but not completely well."

"I see."

"The river? How?…you can't swim?" Sam asked.

"My Grandfather."

"A Hologram?"

"No! I remembered Enoch's prayer. I recited it, and I swear my Grandfather pulled me from the water."

"Right? You prayed?"

"I thought maybe it was time!"

They chuckled together.

Sam stopped laughing and looked deep into her eyes. "I need to know. How much of my dreams and nightmares were your Hologram projections?"

"Just enough to try to keep you away from here."

"At the risk of making me insane!"

"I did not want you dead."

Sam saw Tiye was shivering. He held out his arms. "Survival hug! Captain's orders!"

Tiye held back, moved slowly toward him, then fell into his arms. They held each other quietly, enjoying the warmth of their bodies until doubt cooled their passion, and they broke apart.

Sam tried to find something to say, and so did Tiye.

Tiye put her finger on his lips to hush him. "There is no way I can allay your suspicions, Sam. You either trust me, or you don't – and I can see you don't!" She whispered in his ear.

Sam started to say something before he gave her a look of confirmation, then turned serious. "Tiye? There must be a way to tell a real person from a Hologram!"

"Don't trust me, right?"

"I want to with all my heart."

Tiye held up her fingers. "Touch my fingertips."

"What?"

"Just touch your fingertips to mine."

Sam shrugged and touched all ten of his fingertips to all ten of hers. As he did and looked into her eyes felt a surge of spiritual union that took away all doubt. "I love you." He said as he moved his hands down around her waist and pulled her close.

Tiye held back a moment before she joined him in a long, sweet kiss of love.

When she broke the kiss, she sighed hard.

"Oops! I'm afraid to ask." Sam said.

"I must go back. Sam."

"Pywiack will be safe. Tenya will protect us!"

Tiye looked around for any sign of a gnat or mosquito drone before she replied. "No, Sam. There is no place to run. You were right about the missiles and the volcanoes."

"My, God! He thinks that will save his evil ass?"

"Something about beating God to the draw."

"No world to redeem?"

"I don't understand it all, but the President is there and he will soon have the nuclear codes."

"So, what can two mortals like us do?"

"Maybe his system needs some fine tuning." Tiye grinned.

"You can't go back there."

"I have to, Sam."

Sam took in a deep breath and blew it out hard. "No, you don't have to. It's my quest remember?"

"You have something you want to tell me?"

Sam started to answer but stopped when he saw a mosquito land on a nearby thistle. Tiye followed his eyes and saw it also.

"So come with me to Pywiack, Tiye."

"No! I have to go back and beg Malcolm's forgiveness!" Tiye snapped.

"Then do that crazy woman – and never talk to me again!"

"You are wrong not to join us, Sam. It is the only way to survive and have the Ahwahnee of your dreams."

"No! I would rather die in Pywiack than live one day in your phony paradise."

"You are a stubborn fool, Sam."

"Not so. I am sure Malcolm understands. After all it is his philosophy."

"What?"

"It's better to rule than to serve."

Tiye touched his lips with her index finger and smiled, then turned and walked away.

Sam watched her go and called after her. "Tell my servants that they should only speak what is best. Surely Satan stirs up trouble among them." Sam mused aloud.

"The Koran, Sam?"

"I need all the help I can get."

Tiye paused and looked back. Her eyes met his with hope and fear before she turned and began to walk across the valley toward the Cathedral Spires which was shrouded in a light mist.

Through the mist Sam could see Cathedral Spires. He remembered that James Hutchings named them Cathedral Spires because they appeared like the towers of a Gothic Cathedral.

Sam gasped when he saw Malcolm had transformed them so they resembled the cathedrals at Barcelona, Cologne, and Paris but instead of a cross, the spires were topped with a huge brightly lit swastika. A swastika that cast a shadow toward an elegant Black Oak Tree. As Sam looked at it, he noticed the shadow of the swastika faded away before it could touch the tree. His memory was foggy. He wasn't sure, but this seemed to be the one where he had planted the acorn to grow a tree when he was a small boy. He touched the Golden Acorn and remembered that his mother had made him say a prayer to bless the acorn he planted to bring forth a "tree of life." as all Black Oaks were to the Ahwahnechee. For a moment, an image of her appeared beckoning him to come to the tree.

He smiled at the thought that Malcolm would be there waiting on him with an endless of rain of lies and Holographic surprises. Sam looked at the tree and grinned. Maybe he could come up with a few surprises of his own.

CHAPTER EIGHTEEN

Scientists had predicted the San Andreas fault would split wide open for all recorded geologic time. For hundreds of years, fracturing and weakening of the area around the fault had gone on; it had never fulfilled its potential of doom before today. This day, the fault creep that provided periodic landslides and small earthquakes — ceased. The two giant plates that once moved at the snail's pace of a quarter of an inch a year erupted along the main fault line trace. It split open the length of the fault from San Francisco to Bakersfield. It erupted with such violent movement that it took the Eastern boundary of California and dumped it violently into the sea.

In a matter of minutes, Reno was a seaside resort. A seaside with a legion of Tarmacs rushed inland at a hundred miles an hour, burying Nevada and Northern Arizona in ten billion gallons of seawater. Acidic seawater caused the land it touched to become a field of quick clays and a new ocean bottom devoid of life.

Aftershocks rocked Tuolumne meadows, yet none could be felt inside Cathedral Spires, where Malcolm had built his Temple and Throne room. Hidden behind 9-inch-thick Titanium walls and sunk 66.6 meters into the ground it was more disaster-proof than Norad, which was at this time broken and burning.

Inside, Malcolm's Temple all were safe from the cataclysms of the world outside, but many would have preferred it to being counted among Satan's flock. They were the last of The Keepers who refused the implant and clung to a belief in the Nazarene.

Malcolm looked upon them with rancor as he sat on his Emerald Throne beneath a vaulted ceiling of gold and a cella of the finest crystal. There were seven torches of fire around it, and before it, 144,000 people belonging to different races and genders –but all of one faith who still had not come to worship of their own free will. He had plied them with every comfort and reward they wished for in their wildest dreams. Here they did not have to do anything except enjoy luxurious surroundings and an endless feast. All he asked was they deny God and turn to him. Yet The Keepers refused his gifts, and some fasted until near starvation.

The Red Dragon would not sit on the throne before they kneeled to him or perished. In either case, there would be no one left to be redeemed and no need for Judgment Day.

This day Malcolm was preparing to address The Keeper s and lure them to his stairway to hell. First, he would warm his soul with hellfire. Waving his arm in a circle, he caused flames to appear and found himself in a ring of fire that formed a thirty- foot wall all around him. A fire that burned with intense heat but did not con-sume any fuel. He washed his hands in it as one would wash in a stream of water.

He delighted in the familiar touch.

Seconds later, he pulled the fire to his face. The fire burned away his flesh and formed huge blisters that fell out quickly, leaving behind new skin that formed smooth and unblemished. His eyes sparkled anew, and his hair thickened and grew young.

He loved fire.

In it, he saw death, then renewal.

The Nuclear fires he would soon lose would destroy this world and set the stage for his new earth. A new earth cleansed of all the mealy-mouthed psalm singers that were constant irritants to his being. He would be happy if he never heard another Hallelujah or ever again had to cringe at the sound of a child's prayer.

As he paused and looked into a pool of water, he was very pleased with what he saw. He was delighted to feel a new sense of beauty. The more he changed, the more handsome he thought he became. His face was now that of a gorgeous creature of light. The beauty he had been before they made him a hideous dragon and cast him down.

Now he appeared before The Keepers to the sound of Trumpets, Pomp, and Circumstance. Once the sound faded, he stood before them dressed in his most radiant attire and in his most Christ- like form backed by a band of Glorious Angels who sang inspirational songs before he spoke.

"My Good People! Listen to me! You have been lied to by the Great Deceiver. Not I, as you have been told, but the God you have been on your knees to for countless ages. You have beseeched him with endless prayers but look upon the world outside. It has come to ruin. He gives you famine; I give you feasts. He gives you to ruin, and I give you sanctuary. All I ask is you allow me to vaccinate you against all the diseases of the world. My men will pass among you and will not force you – I ask you to come to me of your own free will – but I advise you to accept this mark of good faith for your own good." Malcolm paused and bowed his head slightly as Attendants dressed in Angelic garb passed among the congregation of the Keepers with JetJects at the ready. As they did, each of the faithful refused the implant, turned away, and knelt in silent prayer.

John, who had gotten another more powerful implant by force, was compelled to move up beside Malcolm.

"Look upon your Leader. He stands with me. Tell them, John!" Malcolm moved aside and let John speak.

A hush fell over The Keepers as John looked out over them. There was visible pain on his face as he began to speak. "Malcolm has given us much for which to be grateful. I...I ask you...to do as he asks. It is little enough to give him thanks for the bounty he has bestowed on us." John stopped and went to his knees in pain. "No! Pray for me that...I...that I might not mock God!"

The Keepers erupted into a chorus of Hosanna's before return- ing to silent prayer.

John fell coiled up in pain.

Malcolm was enraged. "You have chosen this day whom you wish to serve! So, you will die, and your God would have no one left to redeem." Malcolm thundered, and his voice was echoed on amplified devices until all had to cover their ears.

The image of people on their knees praying to heaven brought back painful memories. He was the only Angel with the of the Archangels to cast him out. He loathed Michael. Michael had won a fight on his home court. But Michael was not going to win this time. He would have to fight on Malcolm's playing field and his time – this time. Malcolm felt it was all about jealousy anyway. As Lucifer, the Angel of Light, Lucifer Morningstar he was more beautiful than any of them.

In his mind, even more beautiful than he, who had been his creator.

The Creator, whom he knew, had a timetable for J-Day.

So did Malcolm.

Malcolm shivered slightly as he felt the rustle of familiar feathers. He shivered more as he heard the distant sound of a harp and smelled the incense.

He knew he had to hurry.

CHAPTER NINETEEN

The long night of the winter solstice was a time of feasting in hell. Satan loved the darkness and celebrated the longest night with a suspension of punishments. He was once the most magnificent embodiment of light, but now he despised it. So great was his disdain for it, he ordered all the hellfire tamped down, and even the slightest glimmer of light was not allowed. For this brief period, he wished not to be reminded of the first day of creation and the long summer day when he was cast down.

Michael had often watched this perverse feast as a form of entertainment. He did not watch it this day. Instead, he decided he would help the Guardian Angels who were too few to tend the needs of the countless souls in peril. In so doing he might also forget his temptation to pull the Sword of The Word and end it all now.

Malcolm was still fuming from the faithful Keepers refusing to worship him. He had wanted them to do it of their own free will and really did not understand their refusal. Now he would have them implanted with the latest Chip of Obedience and would bring them to their knees mouthing loud Hosannas. He was happy with that thought until he looked up at a monitor and saw Sam moving towards the Black Oak with an Axe in his hand. He turned and looked at Tiye who was standing beside him. "That damn fool. What is he going to do?"

"With him, one ever knows."

Malcolm grinned and gave her a withering stare. "Is this a fulfillment of your riverside plotting?"

"What?"

"Perhaps one day you will love me as much as you do him?"

"I..."

"Hush! Let's enjoy his little charade." Malcolm insisted as he watched Sam raise the axe to strike the tree.

Sam raised the axe to strike as he looked at a surveillance cam. "Free John and give me Pywiack or I will cut down the tree of life!"

"Are you going to let him cut down the tree of life?" Tiye asked.

Malcolm could barely hold back a smirk and feigned outrage. "No. We must not let that happen." He looked at Tiye with pleading eyes. "Will you go stop him?"

"Me? You know he doesn't listen to me."

"He will now – as he did once before."

"Please, Malcolm! This is not Eden, and I am no Eve."

"No! You are Lillith. Much more powerful and persuasive."

"No, thanks. You broke your promise and implanted The Keepers so maybe we should let Sam end all this with a swing of his axe." Tiye was defiant until she felt a pain in her gut so intense, she went to her knees. She looked at her hands and saw no implant scar. "You promised you wouldn't..."

"Go stop him now of you will feel pain you cannot endure."

Tiye tried to disobey but could not.

Sam stood beneath the majestic Black Oak at the foot of Cathedral Spires. He was about to strike the tree with the axe when he saw Tiye coming his way. He knew Malcolm would have some surprises. At least this was a welcome one.

Tiye watched and waited until Sam lowered the axe before she moved to his side.

Sam turned to see her and almost dropped the axe. "You again?"

"Yep, me again."

"What version of Delilah greets me now?"

"Tiye 101, believe it or not." Tiye reached out with her finger-tips extended.

Sam smiled and touched his fingertips to hers. They paused for a sentimental moment before cold reality came between them.

"And what are your marching orders from Hell's headquarters?" Sam raised the axe to strike the tree.

"Aren't you supposed to protect it, not kill it?" Tiye asked calmly.

"I wasn't going to until he sent you and confirmed how important it must be to his plans." Sam raised the axe.

"Are you not an Ahwahnechee guardian? If you do this, won't you lose your spot in Elo'win?"

Sam lowered the axe and glared at her. "Get behind me Satan!"

Tiye shook her head and looked hurt, then very sad.

"What is this all about, Tiye? I know he's listening, but tell me what's his next move?"

"All I know is I came to tell you; you are still welcome to join us." She winked and hoped he got the message.

"I might just do that. But only if Malcolm frees John and The Keepers and leaves Pywiack to me." Sam paused to smile at her. "Go tell him that."

"You just did."

"Right."

They looked at each other with love and quiet understanding.

Sam picked up an acorn then looked at Tiye. "This isn't the tree of life. Is it?"

"I have no idea. But I don't think the forbidden fruit was acorns."

"What if it once bore the most delicious fruit but now bears bitter fruit to remind us of disappointing God." Sam turned toward Cathedral Spires. "Is that how it was, Malcolm?"

Tiye wondered at the veracity of what Sam was saying. She smiled as she watched a dozen squirrels gather acorns and take them off to their homes. "Yes. I tasted an acorn once. It was very bitter." Tiye looked the acorn over. It had a crack in the shell. She pulled it open and spied a weevil larva wriggling in the seed. "Ugh!" She said as she dropped the acorn.

Sam picked the acorn up, pulled the weevil larvae from the seed, and ate it. "Yum!" He grinned.

"Disgusting!"

"Oh, no! Even better fried in bear fat."

"How about some quinoa and brown rice with garlic sauce and a glass of old vine Zin?"

"Acorns are good food if you bleach and grind them. They go good with Laurel and red ant salad."

"And you know this, how?"

"I am beginning to know myself, Tiye." Sam touched the trunk of the tree, placing the palms of both hands reverently against the bark. He sighed hard, and his knees buckled before he stood tall and smiled. "Tiye, I felt their spirits!"

"Good for you, Sam."

"It *is* the tree of life, Tiye. It provided food for my people and all the creatures of the forest. It is the tree of life for birds, deer, black bears, almost every form of wildlife."

Tiye looked at him and was about to reply when she noticed his face looked different. His cheekbones seemed wider, and his Malibu tan, a little darker. His hair, which had curls, was now perfectly straight. The premature gray was becoming jet black. She wondered if this was a Hologram sent by Malcolm to test her loyalty. She looked hard for any hint of badly encoded pixels or nozzle leakage.

There was none.

Since it wasn't a Hologram, she wondered if Malcolm was right, and Michael was helping Sam.

"The spirit of Tenaya is here. That is what Malcolm fears!"

Sam grabbed her arm and pulled her to the tree. He forced her to touch it with the palms of her hands. "It's real, Tiye! Feel it!" Sam demanded.

"No, Sam. I must go."

"No, Tenaya will protect you, Malcolm cannot harm you!" Sam saw the doubt in her eyes. He pulled her away, and then he put his hands against the bark.

Tiye watched as his cheekbones became smaller, his Malibu tan faded, the curl and premature gray returned to his hair.

Sam pressed harder as his eyes filled with hurt. He pulled back and sighed hard as he looked at Tiye. "They left me."

"I'm sorry…"

"The spirits found me unworthy. It's just a stupid tree." Sam picked up the axe again.

"Isn't this where you planted a tree as a boy?"

Sam paused, put the axe down and looked at the tree with affection. He thought about it and remembered placing the acorn on the ground. He recalled how the sun had cast the shadow of Cathedral Spires so that the tip of the spires formed a cross on the spot where he buried the acorn.

Now the shadows of swastikas where approaching tree.

Sam picked up the axe again. "I can not let evil cast its shadow on it." Sam swung the axe hard. The axe blade hit the tree and shattered. The axe handle disintegrated, and Sam fell back in shock.

"You ok, Sam?"

Sam was stunned for a long moment before he replied. "It isn't just a tree."

Tiye gave him a steely-eyed "no!" She shook off her fear, drew close and spoke in a near whisper. "Neither Malcom nor I sent any Tenaya Holograms. There is a strong Ahwahnee spiritualism in this valley he fears…" The words were barely out of her mouth when she dropped to her knees in pain.

Sam pulled the clovis knife. "Let me ease your pain?"

Tiye got to her feet and held up her hands for him to back away. "I…I am at Malcolm's side of my own free will!"

Sam did not want to believe it but saw no implant scar. "Let me go back with you and talk to him."

"No! Just stay away. Please!" Tiye gave him a tender kiss on the cheek. She let the tips of the fingers on her right hand touched the tips of those on Sam's right hand. The honest tingle told Sam she was not a hologram. "People were cast out of Eden. The book was not. Do not let anyone near it. I love you." Tiye whispered in his ear.

"Wormwood." Sam mused.

"Wormwood?"

"We will find the answer in wormwood. I need fire."

"I have to go."

"No, Tiye. They are telling me my faith is lacking."

"I hope you work it out."

Sam grabbed her hands and looked them over. "He didn't implant you?"

"I came because I care about you." Tiye seemed sincere.

Sam saw the hurt in her eyes and knew Malcolm was controlling her. There was no implant scar, so he had to believe she was under his control out of fear. He wanted to take her hand and run away but knew neither of them were free to do their own will.

"I know the spirits left because I doubted. Wormwood represents your doubts. You destroy them in the fire."

"Do not be deceived, Wormwood. Our cause is never more in danger than when a human, no longer desiring but still intending to do our enemy's will, looks round upon a universe from which every trace of him seems to have vanished and asks why he has been forsaken, and still obeys." Tiye mused.

"Where did that come from?"

"C. S. Lewis."

"Meaning?"

"It just came to mind." Tiye paused and looked worried.

"Yes! When the 7th Seal is opened, Wormwood will make itself known, and the Apocalypse will begin."

"Doesn't there have to be a falling star?"

They looked up at the clear blue sky and shrugged.

"I have said too much. I must go. I do wish you well, Sam." Tiye smiled and turned to leave.

"No! Please wait. I want Malcolm to see the power of Tenaya."

"Sam. Please."

"Just give me a few minutes to find the mug wort and get some more wormwood."

"No, Sam. I need to get back." Tiye paused to grin. "I have to admit I would like to have seen you try a Ghost dance around a fire, Sam."

"You know I'm not a good dancer."

"Oh, I think you will work it out." Tiye insisted. She moved to go and stopped as fiery hailstones began to rain down around them. They ran underneath the shelter of the Black Oak, where no hail fell. As quickly as the hailstones had appeared, they vanished.

"Some trick of Malcolm's?" Sam wondered.

"I don't think so," Tiye replied.

"Aren't you as sick of this cyber world as I?" Sam ran to the tree and pressed his palms against it. He shook with sadness when he felt nothing. He turned and looked at Tiye. He was still suspicious of Tiye but without evidence of an implant he had to imagine she was under threat and fear of her or John's life. He looked at her and looked a little embarrassed. "What a fool I am to believe in miracles."

"Miracles are as easy as a keyboard or verbal mouse." Tiye mused.

"Yes. Step right up, folks. No need to get up for church on Sunday. Punch up the miracle app and the electronic Gods will bestow your heart's desire instantly."

"Except, it is a real miracle that you found yourself."

"Have I?"

"You still feel you do not belong here?"

"How am I to know surrounded by electronic lies. All I know for sure is I am a bastard descendant of the man who destroyed the Ahwahnechee people."

"Not true."

"It's Okay, Tiye. I have known the truth all my life and am now determined to face it."

"No, it is not the truth. We had orientation when I was a summer volunteer at Yosemite. The truth is that after the Mariposa wars, Major Savage took the last of the Ahwahnechee to safety among the Mono Lake Paiutes."

"You mean the dirty dig…"

"They were called that because they were driven from their hunting grounds and found it so hard to find food, some had to dig in the dirt to get the smallest meal."

"Yes, even in my time." Sam grimaced. "But Major Savage, my blood, killed Tenaya!"

"No, Sam. Tenaya was killed by the Paiutes, who accused him of stealing horses. Major Savage took the lan Ahwahnechee Indian Maiden for a wife? She was one of the last of her tribe." Tiye gave him a critical gaze. "I'm sure they loved each other."

"I would like to believe that."

"You are as much Ahwahnechee as any living person." Tiye said and waited for a Pain Impulse. A small one made her flinch.

Sam saw her flinch and suspected an implant – but no implant site was seen. He knew Malcolm was listening and admired her for enduring pain to talk to him. "Well, you can go back and tell, Malcolm I will do no harm to this tree. He didn't need me after all. He knew where I was all along." Sam paused to look a mosquito buzz by. "Right, Malcom?"

They laughed together before they fell into each other's arms and held onto each other in a desperate hug of need not wanting to ever let go.

Sam could feel Tiye's inner struggles resounding in his soul and he was not going to let her go back to Malcolm. She gave him no choice as she broke the hold.

"I have to go."

"I know. So, ahmmm…" Sam stopped as he saw a ring of fire nearby.

As they watched, a raven flew onto a branch just above their head. In its beak was a piece of wormwood. The Raven let it go, and it fell in front of Sam.

Sam picked it up. "Real or Malcolm's?"

Tiye shrugged.

"If the worm can climb the mountain, so can I!" Sam moved to the center of the circle of fire. He looked down and saw many pieces of wormwood. He picked them up with reverence before he was transformed into an Ahwahnechee warrior in ceremonial dress. Suddenly, his feet began to move, and he danced as if he had done it forever. Inside the circle, Sam held the wormwood aloft and danced. He hesitated each time he paused to throw the wormwood in the fire. Suddenly, he found himself surrounded by a dozen Ahwahnechee Warriors motioning for him to throw the wormwood in the fire.

Yet, he could not find the courage to do it.

The Warriors were angry and morphed into Grizzly Bears. Sam stopped dancing and froze. The Grizzlies growled at him with contempt until he gathered the courage to begin dancing again and threw the wormwood into the fire. As the wormwood burned, he felt reborn and like out a whoop of joy!

Tiye saw only a mist, but she heard Sam's whoop of joy. As the mist cleared, she saw Sam approach her smiling.

"Did I dance well enough?"

"There was fog. But I heard your whoops of joy and I see the wormwood is gone."

"It works Ty! I feel no guilt and a sense of freedom I have never felt before. Let me gather some wormwood and you can be free of your guilt."

"That would take a lot of wormwood. Thanks anyway. But I must go."

"No, you don't. He can't harm you! The spirits are strong here."

"For you. Anyway, I'm hungry and it's past dinner time."

"I will get you something to eat."

"Acorn mush? Thanks, but no thanks."

"How about some juicy elderberries. I think I saw a bush on the trail."

"Maybe you could ask your spirits for some real food?"

Sam could barely hold back his anger. "Then go to him and dine at his table. The spirts will tend to me."

"I hope so, Sam. Goodbye."

Sam watched her go and felt a hunger pang himself. He looked up and reached for an acorn on a low hanging branch. As he touched it, it turned into a gorgeous apple. "Tiye, wait. Look!"

Tiye stopped and turned back.

Sam offered her the apple.

Tiye laughed, shook her head, and walked back beside him. "Reversing the roles, Sam?"

"Maybe it's time men took the blame."

Tiye started to reach for the apple. As she did, the shadows from the Cathedral spires crept toward them. As they watched, the darkest shadow of the broken cross, at the top of the spires, moved around their feet.

They both felt a chill unto their souls.

The sound of bone whistles and drums echoed across the valley.

As Sam looked upon it, the apple became worm infested and rotted in his hand. He grimaced, tossed it away and looked up to see Tiye was gone. He felt the intense pain of loneliness once more and was about to abandon all hope.

Then he saw a shooting star fall to the earth.

The Sixth Seal

And I beheld when he had opened the sixth seal, and, lo! There was a great earthquake, and the sun became black as sackcloth of hair, and the moon became as blood. And the stars of the heavens fell unto the earth, even as a fig tree casteth her untimely figs when she is shaken of a mighty wind. And the heavens departed as a scroll when it is rolled together, and every mountain and island were moved out of their places. And the kings of the earth, and the great men, and the rich men, and the chief captains, and the mighty men, and every bondman, and every free man, hid in the dens and in the rocks of the mountains. And said to the mountains and rocks – "Fall on us and hide us from the face of him that sitteth on the throne, and from the wrath of the Lamb. For the great day of his wrath is come, and who shall be able to stand?"

CHAPTER TWENTY

The lithosphere, the atmosphere, and the hydrosphere were all altered into a dynamically interacting system. The system gained energy from the gigantic solar explosions that stormed the sun. The sun's photosphere now ranges from 6000 kelvin to six hundred thousand kelvin. The super-heated wavelengths that fell upon the earth now were, mostly, high-intensity roentgen rays. "X-rays" that penetrated the deep "greenhouse" cloud cover and caused parts of the earth's surface to turn to molten aluminum.

The earth's electromagnetic fields were haywire, and the planet's radiation balance was confused. Geologically, the earth was in the Mesoic era and moving backward. Once more, Mastodons, Tyrannosaurs and thousands of long-extinct beasts roamed the earth once more. Their lifespan was brief as freak cold waves refroze them almost as fast as they thawed.

The Milky Way was in a state of flux with planetary alignment baffling the astronomers but delighting the astrologers.

The United States was now a continental landmass with a seacoast that ran from Moose Jaw, Canada, down to Phoenix on the West coast. The East coast ran from Detroit to Mobile. Icebergs stood off the coasts, sprouting palm trees – palm trees that bore apples and oranges.

A cloud of smelly soot covered the land, pole to pole, with only occasional holes that leaked brilliant, deadly sunlight.

In the smoldering ruins of Paris, it rained cats, dogs, and an occasional cow.

In less than one month after Mother Earth had begun to take her revenge, no human – who held her in contempt – walked the face of the earth.

Except in the Yosemite valley which was now surrounded by encroaching wildfires. Wildfires that stopped just before it reached Yosemites portals.

*   *   *

Sam stood alone by the tree wondering about his next move.

He was not surprised to see Malcolm appear.

"Malcolm? Welcome to the party." Sam mocked. "Here's your tree so I am free to go to Pywiack."

"We both know this isn't the tree, Sam. So, stop the pretense and let's make a deal."

"I thought we decided my soul isn't for sale."

"No, but Pywiack is. Take me to the real tree and it is yours."

Sam paused to think it over. "I don't think you have that power here."

"I think you are drunk on wormwood."

"This is Tenaya's kingdom!"

"Have you been listening to this woman's whispered lies?"

"You are one to talk about lies."

"You believe I can do that without an implant?"

"You have hidden it well."

"She is gaming you, Sam. Her Demon powers are only slightly less than mine!"

There was something about the sincerity in his voice that made Sam doubt. He wanted to believe her, but doubt was creeping into his soul. "Then let her come with me to Pywiack."

"She is free to go where she wishes."

"I think you believe your lies."

"You are making the same mistake Adam did."

"Is that so?"

"Yes. Listening to a woman who is of the lineage of Lillith."

"Really?"

"Who invented the AI generated BVR Holograms, Sam?"

"Who perfected them, Malcolm?"

"I tried but could not because she has embedded encryptions and viruses that are causing all this havoc. It's all a show she is putting on to deceive you. Believe me – she is the evil one. You would be repulsed by her demon self."

"More than yours?"

Malcolm faded in anger for a moment, then reappeared in his Donavan form. "She developed this form to please her lusty desires. She is the one destroying your Ahwahnee, Sam." Malcolm morphed back.

Sam picked up a piece of wormwood lying on the ground. He held it out to Malcolm. "Let's gather some wormwood and have a ritual dance to decide the truth."

Malcolm seemed wary of the wormwood and backed away. "I know you don't believe me. Will you believe your eyes? She has shut down all the systems. Look!" Malcolm thundered, then projected an image of the interior of the Temple where the Keepers were struggling for air. "She has shut down the air intake, and the elevator is locked. All these people will die because of her, not because of me."

Sam watched as some young Keepers seemed to be suffocating in agony. Also, John was struggling for air and looked at him with pleading eyes.

"Come on. It's a setup. Malcolm, turn off that projection and tell the truth!"

"You are more of a fool than Adam was. What is it about this place that makes women into such seducers of men?"

Sam shrugged and began looking around for pieces of wormwood. He picked up a few pieces and they formed a small cross in his hands. "I'll let you know as soon as I can summon the Ahwahnechee angels!"

Malcolm growled in displeasure before he faded into the shadows.

Sam looked at the wormwood and his faith increased. He also gripped the Golden Acorn in his hand, the smell of roasted acorns filled the air and his instinct for truth returned. Whatever Malcolm's plans were, Sam knew he had no intention of restoring Ahwahnee to a new Eden. It had all been a ruse to lure the unsuspecting and The Keepers to Malcolm's Temple. He was still unsure about Tiye but chose to believe she was implanted. He loved her for her bravery. If it was true, she had shut down his systems she had done it to save people, not harm them.

A chilly wind made him shiver, and he was beset by aching loneliness for Tiye. He scoffed at the notion she could be a Demon. He would not let himself believe she would be with Malcolm of her own free will. He considered trying to rescue her but knew that was a suicide mission.

As he pondered what to do next, he thought about the words Tiye had whispered: "Neither Malcom nor I sent any Tenaya Holograms. There is a strong Ahwahnee spiritualism in this valley he fears." She had also said: "People were cast out of Eden. The book was not. Do not let anyone near it."

Tiye had had also told him that even the best BVR Holograms could not replicate the tender tingle of truth found in the touch of true love. The touch of her fingers on his was all he needed to renew his trust in her. Their fingers had touched, and he still had an inner glow from it. It was the real Tiye and she loved him. She had risked pain telling him this, so she was not with Malcolm of her own free will.

Sam smiled when he thought of Malcolm's fear of wormwood. He touched the Golden Acorn and wondered about faith. He had never had it, because faith was based on trust and complete confidence that what you were experiencing was real. It was a belief that was hard to come by in Malcolm's world of dazzling and endless deception. Sam knew John and The Keepers were ready to die to keep the faith in something none of them and ever seen. At least Malcolm's Holocasts were entertaining, could be touched and could be taken as real. What John and his flock had faith in was some ancient writing, a legend of Saints and promises made by a Nazarene who claimed to be the son of God.

Sam's faith depended on tangible proof and, perhaps, held it in his hand. Sam could see and feel wormwood and knew it would keep him safe from evil. He smiled when he thought he would gather a bundle and light a fire in Malcolm's temple. Suddenly he was sure that was what The Ahwahnechee spirits wanted.

His thoughts were interrupted by the rumble of rocks collapsing. He looked in the direction of the sound and saw an opening to a cavern that was not there moments ago. His first instinct was to ignore what he considered a trap Malcolm had set for him. He smiled at that thought as he gathered as much wormwood as he could carry in one hand.

It was time to go into the Red Dragon's lair and end it all one way or the other.

Once inside the cave, Sam peered into the darkness and was gathering his thoughts when a boulder closed the entrance behind him. He knew he was committed to whatever lay ahead now. He was pleasantly surprised to see the humid darkness of the caverns filled with light. His eyes brightened as he looked up at an Amethyst ceiling full of gemstones illuminated by a million pinholes of light streaming down onto a floor that glistened with sapphire blue and emerald, green. There were smooth walls of exquisite marble, laced with seams of gold and streaks of silver, on each side. He looked up to see a spiral tunnel that resembled a lava tube and a marble staircase that led to a large door. When he reached the top of the staircase, he came upon a dark entryway.

As the darkness began to fade, he saw a portal open in front of him. Sam held back a moment, then walked through it. Once on the other side, he was greeted by a mist that smelled of incense cedar and saw a large room carved out of luminous limestone. When the mist faded, he was stunned to see a long valley with a river, filled with fish that had no eyes, running through it. The landscape was arid and flat and devoid of any foliage or mountains and any living thing. Nearby he could see a traditional Ahwahnechee O'chum dwelling with its bark of incense cedar. Outside the O'chum were woven baskets full of berries, various greens, seeds, and acorns. Beside them were scoop baskets with dried fish and some deer meat hung out to dry. Close by, there were spears with obsidian points and mahogany shafts.

Sam walked up to the O'chum entrance, peeked inside, then entered the O'chum. It was dark inside, but he sensed he was not alone.

"Even now it may be too late." A voice came out of the shadows.

Sam's sensed a Hologram and decided to play along. "Ok, Malcolm. Let's see the show." There was no reply. Then, from the darkness came a loud resounding roar. It echoed throughout the cave and caused him to stop. It sounded even louder once more, and before the echoes faded, a huge Grizzly Bear bounded out of the darkness.

Sam sensed this was no hologram, so he backed up until he was against the wall with nowhere to go.

The Grizzly Bear loped toward him; his sharp teeth covered with hungry foam. Once it was close enough for him to feel its angry breath, Sam went down to his knees. "Oh, great, Yosemite. We bow humbly before you."

The Grizzly Bear roared even louder and snarled, baring his fangs close to Sam's face. Sam strained with all his courage not to show weakness. "I swear before the El-o'-win, I have never harmed you and never tasted your flesh."

The Grizzly sniffed Sam all over roared once more before it faded into a mist.

Sam sighed in relief until he saw a vision of his mother, Totuya dying in a hospital bed. As she lay in the Hospice bed dying all alone, she held the worn beads of a Rosary in her weathered hands. The rosary beads were made of hard green, Black Oak acorns, and had an empty clasp that had once held a Golden Acorn.

Sam stood in the shadows for a long moment before turning to walk away. He was stopped by a Nurse.

"Are you here to see someone, sir?"

Sam hesitated before replying. "No! No, I don't know…" He stopped and looked at his mother's kind eyes. "Yes, she is my mother."

The nurse left, and Sam approached his mother's bedside. He stood there quietly before she reached out and took his hand. With her touch, he felt her familiar warmth and knew this was not a hologram.

"Even now it may be too late, my son." Totuya said.

"For me to repent and say I am sorry?"

"No! To save the land."

"Yes, Mother. I helped the evil one destroy Ahwahnee. If I forfeit my life – will I be forgiven?"

"First, forgive me."

Sam's hesitated to reply. His mother had bright young eyes, but her face was world-weary, and her voice thundered with truth. "Mother, you have done nothing to be forgiven for."

"We were outcasts, called names and lived in poverty. I know you wanted to live a better life. I failed to give it to you."

"I ran away and denied you and all my people."

"Yet the Great Spirit still abides in you."

"The savage Black Dog abides there also." Sam looked away from Totuya.

Totuya handed him a bowl of acorn mush. "Eat!"

"I am not hungry."

"There is truth in wormwood but more truth in the fruit of life. "Eat now, my son!"

Sam put down the wormwood, took the bowl and ate the mush in small spoonful's, choking it down and feeling an overwhelming bitterness with each bite. When he stopped eating, he looked up to see a handsome man dressed in a Major's uniform of the United States Mariposa Brigade of the 1850s. The Major held the hand of a beautiful Ahwahnechee Maiden. They smiled as they looked upon a young baby boy swaddled in a woven blanket on a cradleboard.

"Which world should we give him?" Major Savage asked.

"I do not know if he will be welcomed into either of them." The Indian Maiden replied.

"As we are not."

"Where will we go?"

"I don't know. Your father, Tenaya is dead, and they blamed me. We must leave Yosemite now."

"Yosemite? That is a Miwok slur."

"Yes, this is Ahwahnee. We must hurry."

The Indian Maiden nodded, then took a necklace with a Golden Acorn on it and put it around the baby's neck."

"Where did you get that."

"From my father."

"Yes. Did the Medicine man make it for him?"

"No, it was found beneath the sacred tree. It was meant to protect he who will come to restore the valley." The Indian Maiden touched the Golden Acorn. "There will be refuge only when Tutockahnula, Tissaack, and Tokoya stand guard over us, as we were in the beginning."

Major Savage put this arm around her.

A Black Dog howled; the vision ended.

Sam touched the Golden Acorn. "Then this is not a trinket?"

"Without faith, it is but a pleasant adornment." Totuya said. "And with faith?"

"It will restore Ahwahnee."

"Restore Ahwahnee? How? How am I to…."

"Deny The Black Dog. Cleanse your spirit. Keep the Faith."

"Please! Can't you tell me exactly…"

"The Black Dog is the hatred you harbor for both peoples in your heart. No amount of wormwood or ritual dance can cleanse you of that."

"Yes. I despise all people but not as much as I despise myself."

"Have faith in love. If you do not, The Black Dog will devour you."

"No! Love is the greatest deception of all!"

"Not true love."

"How does one know it?"

"It enters through the heart but endures through the spirit."

"I have not known it."

"There is one your spirit knows you love."

"Tiye? No, she is not to be trusted."

"She is not what the Evil One would have you believe. Cast doubt from your heart. She will help you fulfill your destiny."

"My destiny? What…"

"Go swiftly. There is not much time."

"Go where? Do what? Please!"

"Go to Pywiack. Bathe in the cleansing waters and purge hatred from your soul. Listen to the winds and all will be made known to you." Totuya faded, and a vision of Ahwahnee, as the Paradise it was in the beginning, appeared.

Sam looked upon happy people who found food in abundance for all. The rivers gave them plenty of fish, and the meadows, sweet clovers, and other edible roots in abundance. The flora yielded acorns, pine nuts, fruits, and berries. In the forests were herds of deer and other animals, which gave meat for food and skins for clothing and beds. Here they lived in peace and worshipped the Great Spirit, which gave them life. They made no graven images or raised no altars to The Great Spirit. The Great Spirit was in all living things, and if they treated all life with reverence. They believed that, even in death, their spirits would return to dwell forever in Ahwahnee.

This day, they romped with joy beneatha cloudless sky of deep blue, and the air was soft and sweet. The animals seemed particularly friendly, and everyone was in a good mood. Many played music on bone whistles and danced with boundless delight.

It was indeed an Eden.

Sam felt sad as he looked upon it but was shaken by the sound of thunder that drove him to his knees. He looked up to see the skies full of flaming clouds shaped like swords. People ran before them toward the East portal, and in a brief time, the valley was devoid of all life. All that remained was a majestic Black Oak laden with ripe fruits that morphed into acorns.

Moments later, a legion of Ahwahnechee Cherubim's carrying a Golden Book with seven seals disappeared beneath the Black Oak tree. They placed it on an alabaster altar and stood guard beside it. They seemed to fade as Tiye walked up to the altar and touched the book.

Upon her touch, the earth and all upon it vanished in flames. Then the vision vanished, and Sam was by himself in the cave holding a bone whistle in his hand. He looked at it and smiled. It wasn't much, but he took it as a sign that what he had seen was not a Hologram but a message from the Great Spirit. He was not sure what it all meant but he felt a blossom of faith in his soul. He put the bone whistle in his mouth and blew it.

The piccolo sound echoed in the cavern; then, there was quiet.

"You want to stop that infernal noise, Sam? "Malcolm, in his most handsome morph, demanded.

"You?" Sam picked up the wormwood.

Satan laughed. "Go ahead light a fire and let's have a ritual dance." Sran took a piece of wormwood and gave it a mocking kiss.

Sam put his wormwood down.

"How do you like my latest generation of holograms, Sam? I thought you might like to see your mother one more time to make peace with her."

"No! She was real. This bone whistle is real."

"5D printing on-demand and at any place desired. Want me to make a dozen?"

"You are here to cast doubt." Sam touched the Golden Acorn. "I believe this is more than just a trinket."

Malcolm waved his hand, and a reflecting pool appeared beside them. He admired himself in the reflecting pool, then gave Sam a look of respect. "Let's talk like old friends."

"Not until we have finished our business."

"Our business?"

"Let Tiye go. You have the entire world. Why do you need her?"

"There is no fire in hell, hot enough to consume loneliness, Sam." Malcolm looked sad. "I will free her, but not until it is time." "It's past time. Do it now!"

"No, Sam. It's the fifth time. The predicted time. The end time. The time for me to win! "Malcolm morphed into a Red Dragon with a hideous countenance. He stood before Sam, surrounded by evil penetrating darkness and the pervasive stink of pestilence. The air smelled of sulfur, and the cries of the damned echoed throughout the cavern. Lightning and thunder rocked the cave.

"Kudos to your CGI guys, Malcolm." Sam scoffed. "Now, can you let Tiye go?"

Malcolm morphed back to his angelic self. "Tiye? A name for a Queen. I have asked her to be my bride again and share the new Eden to come." Malcolm morphed into his most handsome self, dressed in the best GQ array. "Instead, she infected my system with a doomsday virus, and she will not be freed until she has removed it!"

"I hope she will find the courage not to do that?"

"Sam, you still think of me as evil?" Malcolm looked for a hint of kindness from Sam. "Soon, the old world will be gone. I shall create a whole new one, a world with no stop signs where everything goes, and there is no need for maddening prayers or supplicating to the heavens. Is that evil?" Malcolm swelled with pride.

"I think you know the answer to that!"

"Good and evil are relative things, wouldn't you say, Sam?"

"No! Mister Mephistopheles, I would not!"

"Wrong, Sam. Lucifer Morningstar, The angel of light. The most beautiful thing in all creation." He paused once more to admire himself in a reflecting pool. "I was more beautiful even than he that made me."

"I don't think that attitude was very popular with your creator."

"Oh? Was it not evil to condemn me for beauty that was not of my making?"

"Take it up with him."

"I intend to, very soon."

"Tiye will not do what you have planned for her."

"Which is?"

"She is of the lineage of David. You want her to open the book."

"Book?"

"You didn't need me to find it. You knew where it was all along."

"Of course. I was there when it was closed and sealed."

"The Ahwahnechee Angels will not let her or anyone else but the worthy one touch the book."

"My Nephilim will see to the Ahwahnechee cherubim."

"Not even you have that power." Sam hoped.

"Perhaps not, but with your help it might work out."

"Ha! I wouldn't help you across the street."

"I can only use those who seek to be used, Sam. Look into yourself."

"Well, I think, and you are going to get yours!"

Malcolm flinched and looked scared for a moment. "So, do you blame me for doing anything I can to prevent it?"

"I don't care what you do! Leave Ahwahnee out of it."

"Why? You never belonged here."

"So that hologram with my mother was another lie?"

"A gift to an old friend. I hope you enjoyed it."

Sam held the bone whistle tight. "No! I don't believe anything you say."

"You call me a lair but your whole life is a lie, Sam!"

"Not like you!"

"For all that is said of me – it cannot be said that I ever lied about who I am."

The truth of those words stung Sam. "I...."

"You are as much an outcast as I!"

"I am nothing like you!"

"You believe all that is said about me?"

"Yes."

"I have always been on your side."

"Now that's the lie of all lies!"

"No, Sam. I have always wanted you to be happy. In honor of the friendship we once had, did I not offer you your heart's desire."

"A holographic Ahwahnee? No, thanks."

"A state-of-the-art gift for you to enjoy. That is all I have ever wanted for you and even for those who curse me."

"What about The Keepers and Tiye?"

"I have given The Keepers a sanctuary, and as to Tiye, I just removed a virus she placed in my systems that shut them down."

"So? If they were not working, when I saw Totuya..." Sam started to put the bone whistle in his mouth. "And the dance was real also!"

"Careful, Sam."

"Here, you have no power over me, do you?"

"I do not want to destroy you unless you make me."

Sam held the bone whistle in one hand and clasped the Golden Acorn in the other.

Satan looked worried.

Moments later, Tiye appeared in a Holocast. She was locked in a Computer Servo room surrounded by an endless row of Server Racks and a bank of Holographic Virtual Servers. Several ZZ Robo goons and a few Facista "technicians" moved about around her.

"Look, Sam. She is unharmed working hard on your virtual Ahwahnee." Malcolm offered.

"How are you, Ty?" Sam asked.

"I'm sure he has filled you in." Tiye's voice reeked of sarcasm.

"I guess you planted some kind of virus that was messing up his works."

"I was wrong. I have removed it and am working hard at making us a paradise, Sam."

"Are you in pain?"

Tiye gave him a half nod looking scared. "Sam, you were right about the seven volcanoes! He intends..." Tiye grimaced and doubled over the Holocast vanished.

"Damn you, Malcolm! Leave her alone."

"Perhaps I will when her usefulness is ended." Malcolm projected a Holocast showing John and The Keepers in the Temple, gasping for breath, along with close-up of children appearing to die of suffocation. "They will all die, and it will be on you if you dare oppose me anymore."

"You will have to kill me to stop me."

"So be it!" Malcolm morphed to the Red Dragon and Sam was surrounded by a raging fire. It burned closer and closer and was depleting the oxygen so he could hardly breath. He was weak but found the strength to put the bone whistle in his mouth. He struggled for the breath to blow it and found only enough for it to make a short sharp sound.

It was enough to dispel the fire and cause Malcolm to vanish.

Sam held the bone whistle with delight and touched the Golden Acorn with reverence. "I am not good at this faith thing. But something I can hold on to like this certainly helps! I humbly ask the Great Spirit to guide my hand and give him the grace to have the faith and the wisdom on how to proceed."

There was only the faint echo of his prayer, then his mother, as a beautiful young maiden, appeared out of the mist. She was dressed in celestial raiment and fitted with rudimentary angelic wings. "Look upon me and believe my son."

"Mother, are you an angel?"

"In training. There is much to learn before one can grow wings."

"Yes. I guess I would never make it."

"Your faith is blossoming."

"My world is so full of evil electronic wizardry; what can anyone have faith in it?"

"The seed of faith is found in forgiveness. You are almost there. Go bathe in the holy water of Pywiack. Think of others and deny yourself. Open your heart to love and your mind to the truth."

"I will. I promise. Then you will guide my path?"

"It will all be known to you." Totuya faded.

After she vanished, Sam felt a warmth of self and purpose he had Never felt before. His faith was now in full bloom, and he felt ready to go into the Lion's Den.

Sam had no way of knowing Michael was wary of helping anymore and Sam would be going into the lion's den alone.

The Seventh Seal

"And when he had opened the seventh seal, there was silence in heaven about the space of half an hour. And I saw the seven angels which stood before God, and to them were given seven trumpets. And another angel came and stood at the altar, having a golden censer; and there was given unto him much incense, that he should offer [it] with the prayers of all saints upon the golden altar which was before the throne. And the smoke of the incense, [which came] with the prayers of the saints, ascended before God, out of the angel's hand. And the angel took the censer, and filled it with the fire of the altar, and cast into the earth: and there were voices, and thundering, and lightning, and an earthquake. And the seven angels which had the seven trumpets prepared themselves to sound.

CHAPTER TWENTY-ONE

"So, tell me, Miles, when do I get to meet our benefactor?" Kate asked as she looked out a panoramic window at the golden streets and glittering decor of Malcolm's Throne Room.

"He set it up for 1400. It's almost that time."

"I knew he had accumulated great wealth, but this – this is incredible."

"Yes. I think a little too gaudy for my tastes."

"I agree." Kate sighed. "Did you check to see if the people on my list made it?"

Miles looked sad as he remembered seeing a BVR monitor displaying all those she named being made to worship Malcolm or die. Most had died. He had kept that from her. "I...I will check on it."

"It's okay. I have no illusions about this place. So, did you get your family on board?"

"Ma'am, it didn't seem right to displace three key scientists and a Rabbi for my wife and kids."

"I'm sorry, Miles." Kate looked puzzled. "So, you found a Rabbi?"

"Rabbi Isaac. He's the Kabbalist like you who believes Yeshua is the Messiah and will soon return."

"Isn't Rabbi Isaac over a hundred years old?"

"Yes, but he is very spry."

Kate shook her head and looked cynical. "Miles, I am disappointed in you. I wanted no favors."

"You always said you wanted to meet him."

"Thank you, but…" Kate motioned toward a BVR monitor and sighed hard as a satellite feed showed Monterey and Carmel breaking up and sliding into the Bay. "No! Monterrey? No!"

"Your birthplace. I am sorry, Ma'am."

The feed switched to tornadoes in Kansas that came in clusters carrying 300 MPH winds and blew all in their path away leaving the earth behind them devoid of any sign of human habitation.

"Dorothy isn't in Kansas anymore." Kate forced a chuckle.

"Kansas isn't in Kansas anymore." Miles looked at the monitors with hurt in his eyes.

"Your home. Sorry." Kate sighed. "What does our latest intelligence tell us about who's left in the world outside?" Kate pondered sadly.

"I'm sorry, Ma'am. Some of the satellite feeds are garbled, so there is really no way of knowing for sure but seems there is tribulation, famine, and pestilence everywhere but here. The good news is that the Magma here has been stable as our host promised." Miles said as he pulled down a double scotch.

"The Rabbi? You think he could lead us in a non- denominational prayer."

"Ma'am?"

"I would like his blessing."

Miles paused and looked sheepish. "Ma'am, you know Malcolm has prohibited any prayer except to him. His men have confiscated all religious symbols and just had a bonfire of Bibles and a lot of very sacred relics."

"You believe he is the anti-Christ?"

"If such a person exists, he fits the bill."

"…so, these are the so-called, end-times?"

"I'm no biblical scholar, but many signs are there."

"Perhaps it's the earth finally tired of our abuse."

"A new earth is part of the end-times predictions."

"Perhaps it will be better off without us?"

"Maybe, but it is not a good thing for Malcolm – if he is the anti-Christ."

"Yes, the bottomless pit." Kate paused to smile. "He might try to do everything to avoid that?"

Miles nodded.

They shared a disquieting moment of understanding.

"Well, Miles. I do not intend to join his worship services."

"We might have to."

"No. Never!"

"Everyone must kneel before his throne, or they will not be admitted to the food stores."

"What?"

"I'm sorry, Ma'am. I wish there were somewhere else to go.

Kate shook her head sadly. "Yes. It was beautiful when I first saw it as a young girl. He picked a good spot to build a redoubt."

"Some say it is protected by an old Ahwahnechee curse. Others that it is Eden."

"Whatever he is up to, it isn't about the end times. People have been predicting that for thousands of years."

"Yes, but never before have we had the means to do it." Miles insisted.

Kate touched her left forearm and looked worried. "You think?"

Miles gave her a worried nod.

"You are very religious, aren't you, Miles?"

"I was not until lately. You, Ma'am?"

"More spiritual."

"I know Kabala."

"You'll have to excuse me for a while, Miles." Kate retrieved a yoga mat and began to stretch.

"Oh, yes. Just yell if you need me." Miles moved to open the door. He hesitated a moment, then turned and looked at her with respect.

"Something else, Miles?"

"I didn't vote for you, but I'm glad they elected you. That's all, Ma'am."

"I was not elected, Miles. My predecessors were killed or died in the Pandemic. I am an accidental President, Remember?"

"Well, I would have voted for you."

"Let's hope you get that chance," Kate said as she unfolded her Yoga mat and spread it out.

Miles looked at her with deep admiration. Then they both laughed together. They were stopped by a knock on the door. Miles hesitated to answer. Kate motioned for him to do it. Miles opened the door to see Rabbi Issac standing there.

The Rabbi was Ebony Black with classic Ethiopian features. He had a kind face and elegant bearing.

"I'm Kate." She extended her hand.

The Rabbi slightly bowed.

"I'm Miles," Miles said as he pulled up a chair for the Rabbi.

The Rabbi nodded and passed the chair to sit on Kate's yoga mat in a Buddha pose. He smiled at Kate and patted the rug. "Here. Please sit beside me."

Kate hesitated and kneeled, then finally assumed a yogi position across from him.

"I'll take a walk, Ma'am. Ok?" Miles said as he picked up the "football," clapped the chain to a handcuff on his wrist and moved out the door.

"He is welcome to stay." Rabbi Isaac chortled.

Miles was out the door and did not reply.

Once Miles was gone, the Rabbi and Kate sat quietly, looking at each other. "I know why you hunger, Kate." The Rabbi broke the ice.

"You do?"

"All faiths have left you in darkness."

"I..."

"The root of suffering is attachment."

"I'm not sure I understand?"

"You are on the right path. Turn your back on the useless rites of religions that leave your spirit wanting."

"I find peace in meditation."

"I am happy you are set on the right path."

"You are a Rabbi?"

"I was. But, found it lacking."

Kate looked suspicious. "You lost your faith in God?"

"Have you not?'

"I..."

"Was not your husband and your three children killed by an act of God? A God who invented evil so he could be seen as pure?"

"It was an earthquake. I should have been home with them."

"Ask yourself. If indeed this world was created by God, then there should be no sorrow or evil since all deeds, both pure and impure, must come from him."

"I think we all have the free will to choose between good and evil."

"Free will. His greatest mistake."

"What?"

"Nothing! Look, I am here for your spiritual well-being; you must abandon the heresy of worshiping God. Look about you and ask if a billion prayers have ended this Holocast?"

"Look, I'm really anxious for a meditation period Can we talk later?"

"Perhaps you would find comfort in holding onto something real." He handed her a miniature Golden Calf.

Kate looked it over; shook her head and handed it back. "I need to forget all finite things and concentrate on the infinite. Please!"

The Rabbi looked a little angry then broke into a forced grin. "You are trusting Hermeneutic mysticism when you could put your trust in our benefactor."

The invisible stench of evil seemed to surround Kate.

"Please thank Malcolm for providing a safe haven, but I ask to be excused from his worship services."

"He will not grant that to anyone who wishes to remain here."

"Maybe it was wrong for me to come here."

"There is no other haven."

"It doesn't matter."

"Where would you go?"

Kate stood up and glared at him. "Who are you?"

Rabbi Isaac feigned shock. "I am..."

"No! Tell your master that what he wants will be of no use to him if any harm comes to me."

"I don't know what you are talking about?"

"I would die before I would let him use them."

"Use them? I am a Rabbi here to help guides you on a spiritual awakening…"

"No, Kate! No! He's not a Rabbi." Miles ran into the room. "The einsatz Goons just crucified the real Rabbi Isaac, and they are killing anyone who was known to associate with him.

Kate glared at the Rabbi. "So, who are you?"

"You will soon know all and regret you did not do as I asked." He got up and stomped out of the room.

Kate and Miles watched him go and both shuddered.

"What did you tell him?" Miles asked.

"Not what he wanted to know."

They both looked scared as they listened to the sound of Jack's boots coming their way.

Kate gave Miles a stern look. "Is there any way he can set off those missiles without my bio- rhythms in tune?"

Miles grimaced and looked sad.

"Tell me!"

"In case of your death…well if he has the "biscuit" index." "In plain English!"

"He could send EAMS to the NMCC announcing…you are… that you can't…."

"Miles!"

"Oh? Sorry. He would send Emergency Action Messages to the Military Command Center, giving the actual launch orders. These messages would go to the officers in the various underground Launch Control Centers who would launch US land-based missiles."

"Wouldn't these officers know the messages were false?"

Miles thought it over and shook his head. "Not if he has found a way to send codes that launch crews can confirm by comparing it to codes they have in their SAS."

"Sealed authentication system?"

"Yes."

"I remember the briefing."

Miles looked at her with tears forming in his eyes.

"It's okay, Miles. He has not won yet!"

Miles had to look away to hide his tears.

Kate kneeled on her yoga mat, then reached out to Miles. "Please come pray with me!"

Miles nodded, smiled, and knelt beside her.

CHAPTER TWENTY-TWO

am stood naked in the middle of the Pywiack Cascade. The water was so pure and cool it was ambrosia to the taste and refreshing to the soul. It was a ritual cleansing of his body and soul so that he might be worthy to expel evil from Ahwahnee and take his place in Elo'win. As the water poured over him, he felt the Black Dog awake. He looked to the heavens and hoped for his mother and Tenaya's forgiveness.

The Black Dog awoke in agony snarling at Sam's will to be rid of him. It gnawed at Sam's gut and growled at his every pure thought. The pain was so intense Sam almost left the cascade. Instead, he forced himself to forget all hatred and focus on the things he loved. The Black Dog growled with displeasure. Sam willed it to run. There was an agony that tore at his whole body as The Black Dog sent biting pains deep into Sam's will. Sam was almost at the point of not enduring the pain when he saw a vision of a fire and Ghost dancers. He looked at his right hand to see a piece of wormwood. He was weak from pain but managed to throw it the fire. There was a moment of intense pain that took him to his knees before The Black Dog leaped from his body and was dissolved in the holy water.

Seconds after The Black Dog was gone, Sam felt his strength return tenfold and his soul was at a peace beyond understanding.

Once he was cleansed, he dressed and was pleased to see an O'chum close by. He smiled at this gift from Tenaya, walked toward it and took some Black Oak acorns from a Chuckah basket. He moved to a granite rock, picked up a stone mallet, and began cracking and shelling acorns. Once the shells were gone, he pounded them into a fine yellow meal, poured some water on it, and stirred. Then he took a wooden spoon, filled it with mush, and garnished it with a few Pandora moth caterpillars. He picked one up and threw it down his throat. Nearby was a table full of woven baskets containing mushrooms, berries, squaw root, Miner's lettuce with red ants running over it, their formic acid giving it a pleasant vinegary taste.

After he ate, Sam sat outside the O'chum on a soft blanketof rabbit skin, enjoying the pleasing smell of incense cedar. He was now dressed in Buckskin clothes and moccasins. He looked up to see Tutockahnula, Tissaack, and Tokoya in untouched glory guarding the valley once more. Deer, coyote, Grizzly and Black Bear filled the valley and would come close to being petted. He lay against the trunk of a Black Oak and breathed in the air so pure his breathing was too shallow to feel. He nibbled on berries, nuts, and Kachavee pupa as he fed a handful of Brake Fern to a young mule deer fawn.

It was Idyllic, and he was at peace with himself though he knew this was a blessed interlude to rest him before he confronted Satan.

Somehow his quest had become more evident. From what little Tiye had been able to say, he knew Malcolm intended to use the Tsar Bomb to cause the eruption of the seven super volcanoes. Castle Bravo 666. The Tsar Bomb that was tested in the Arctic, had destroyed houses hundreds of miles from ground zero and broke windows in Norway and Finland. He sighed hard as he knew Kate was Malcolm's captive, and Malcolm would soon have the codes to set those missiles off.

Tiye had gummed up the works, but Malcolm may be able to get past her virus soon. Sam did not know exactly how he would stop it, but he knew he had to try. As he pondered these thoughts, he spied a sinew backed Ahwahnechee bow and a quiver full of wild rosewood arrows with razor-sharp Obsidian tips. He pulled an arrow from the quiver. He ran his finger over the Obsidian arrow point. It drew a small amount of blood.

"Sharper than a surgeon's scalpel," Sam said as he watched the small drop of his blood on the arrow tip. He got to his feet and looked toward a darkening sky. When he looked back, he saw a Beautiful Indian Maiden dressed in buckskin standing in an aura of light.

The Indian Maiden drew close. He knew it was his mother as a young maiden. "Please be at peace." She spoke.

"I am, Mother. You look so young and beautiful."

"I am as I was before the time of troubles."

"Thank you for the gift of this time and place."

"In your faith and forgiveness, Heaven has seen your tears."

"Thank you, Mother. Can I stay here a while longer?"

Totuya gave him a sweet kiss on the forehead. "No, my son! You have much to do."

"I know. I must go into the Lion's Den!" Sam paused. "Yet I am no Daniel. He was beloved by God."

"As, are you?"

"I am underserving...'

"That is a judgement for the Great Spirit to make."

"I am chosen?"

"Yes. You must not let The Evil One defile the Three Graces or the Book of Life. You must make haste to stop the great deceiver. He wishes to rule from the holy mountain, Poo- see- na-chuck- ka set aside for God."

"He has a great Temple there. I will go destroy it."

"No! That is for Judgement Day. You must stop anyone but the worthy one to touch the Book at the appointed time – or evil will prevail."

"The Book of Life? But I don't know where..."

"It will be known to you."

"He knows where it is?"

"As from the beginning."

"Is it not protected by the Ahwahnechee Angels?"

"They can guard against the Evil one. Not one of the lineage of David. You must go to it, for you are the only one who can stop the unworthy one from touching the book."

"Whoever it is, I will kill them before I let that happen."

"Be strong and do not weaken in her presence."

"Her?" Sam swallowed hard. "You don't mean, Ty?"

"He will see that she does his will."

"But I can't kill Ty?"

"She must not touch the book!"

"But mother! Where? How? I..."

"She must not touch the book!" Totuya repeated in a thunderous tone then disappeared leaving Sam wondering exactly what to do.

Sam stood quietly for a long moment. He shook off the notion that Tiye would have to be killed. and convinced himself that if he killed Malcolm, it would all end. Then he armed himself with the sinew backed Ahwahnechee Bow and a quiver full of wild rosewood arrows with the razor-sharp Obsidian tips and put the Clovis knife in his belt. He started to leave the O'Chum, but stopped, looked back, and picked up the bone whistle he had almost left behind.

As if he knew exactly where to go and what to do, Sam almost ran as he headed to a remote back cave entrance that led into Malcolm's Temple. He stopped when he saw it was guarded by two Giant Nephilim.

The Nephilim were huge with bulging muscles, hands large enough to crush a human head with one grip and a look of withering evil on their faces. As Sam moved toward them, they picked up huge boulders and threw them at him. He barely ducked out of the way in time. The Nephilim picked up even larger boulders and were about to toss them, when Sam pulled an arrow frow his quiver, loaded his bow and loosed it. The arrow struck one Nephilim and he vaporized. The other Nephilim saw that and rushed Sam. He was too quick for Sam to reload this bow, so he pulled the Clovis knife. The Nephilim reached for Sam's throat. His huge hands were inches from Sam's throat when Sam drove the obsidian knife into the Nephilim's heart. He vaporized also.

The way in was now open.

Sam gathered his thoughts and looked inside. It was dark and foreboding with the scent of rotted evil in the air. He ignored the darkness and went forth with an unshakeable sense of purpose.

Once inside, Sam stood in the darkness, not sure which way to turn. It seemed to get colder, but he did not shiver from the cold. He was ready to enter The Lion's Den, and even though there still appeared to be no openings, he waited. He knew the first test of faith was to wait. He was a little uneasy until he heard the music.

"Lucifer, our God of ages. Let me hide myself in thee..." It was being sung by a choir and echoed from some distance down the cave where a small beam of light beckoned him. He felt warm as he moved toward it. When he got to a small opening, he could look in on the inside of Malcolm's huge, ornate Tabernacle. There was a choir singing and to the left of the choir was John Pattos standing by a Preacher's Podium conducting a religious service.

The Choir finished the song, and John moved to the podium. "My good people, I know some doubt our holy benefactor, Lucifer Morningstar, but look around you. Is this not a magnificent tabernacle, and has he not allowed us to worship freely in it? The world outside is in chaos, but here we find peace and sanctuary. Let's bow our heads and say a prayer of thanksgiving for our savior Malcolm Mabius."

The 144,000 Keepers did not bow at first.

Malcolm motioned to a nearby Facista at a control panel.

The Facista sent an, megaIPI that sent the Keepers to their knees.

Malcolm smiled as Tiye moved up and stood at his side. He put his arm around her and smiled. "It is done. There will not be a single prayer lifted to the Nazarene and no souls here to be redeemed."

Tiye smiled back, looked at him with love, and gave him a peck on the cheek.

Satan blushed.

"So, there is no more to be done?" Tiye asked.

"All except the final cleansing of the world outside and your breaking of the seals."

"Seals? Which ones would that be?" She teased.

"Now, Lillith! You know more about that, than I do."

Tiye offered a look of innocence.

Satan smiled.

"How do we get past the gatekeeper?" Tiye wondered.

"He will invite you in."

"He will not get past the Nephilim."

"I have seen to it that he already has."

Tiye had to fight off a smile of relief.

"Did I see a moment of love light in those beautiful eyes, my queen?"

"I…"

"Just tell me where you are on Kate?" Malcolm demanded.

"I am close, but the encryption is way past anything I have ever seen," Tiye replied. "We need to hurry! I need for all missiles to fly at once!"

"Can't an implant compel her to give them up?"

"No! It's tied to her biorhythms and linked to a mood monitor. It's that damn free-will app some true believer developed." Malcolm gave Tiye a forceful gaze. "How long will it take you to break the encryptions?"

"I…I hope soon."

"Soon is not soon enough. If you had the chips containing the codes independently of her, would that expedite things?"

"Yes. I scanned her arm, but she blocked it with her thoughts."

Malcolm thought it over and grinned. He turned to Ilse, who was nearby. "Send in Oskar and a Mengele team. If she does not give them up – cut off her arm!"

"No! Just give me a little more time," Tiye spoke up.

Malcolm looked at the doomsday clock, which read: 11:59:59.

"There is no more time!" Malcolm glared at Tiye. "I will take care of Kate. In case I can't, you must go to the tree now and do not fail me!"

Tiye hesitated until she heard a cry of pain from hundreds of Keepers and saw the look of agony on John's face.

CHAPTER TWENTY-THREE

A Squad of einsatz gruppe ZZ Goons burst through the door and held Kate and Miles at gunpoint. They were poised to fire when a machine gun blast from behind cut them down. Kate looked up to see a young Seal Team Major standing in the doorway holding a smoking machine gun.

"We have to move fast, Madame President." The Major said politely.

"What? Who are you?" Kate gasped, and her eyes misted as she looked out on the brightly lit Temple floor that was strewn with thousands of bodies lying at the feet of the Golden Calf. She watched as einsatz gruppe ZZ Goons were throwing the bodies into ovens fitted with powerful lasers that incinerated them instantly. She allowed herself a moment of sadness when she saw Rabbi Isaac's body nailed to a cross upside down. She studied the Major's face and smiled. "Do I know you?"

"I resemble my father. General Richard Zalar."

"Oh, yes!"

"He served with you in the Golan Heights campaign."

"Yes! A good soldier and a good man!" Kate remembered. "Yes, Ma'am!"

"You can be proud of him. He...I'm sorry, he died trying to save his men."

"I know, Ma'am. You were wounded trying to get to him. That is why I am here,"

"How did you get past the Goons?"

"Seal team, Ma'am! The last of a SOG assigned for Presidential protection."

"I was never told about...."

"Secrecy was the key to our survival. Please! We must hurry."

"Yes. Where are we going?"

"There is a small problem, Ma'am."

"Oh?"

"The codes."

"I did not give them up."

"I know. But Malcolm's Techies have almost hacked into them. He intends to set them off. We need to send a deactivation signal now!"

Miles pulled Kate back and whispered in her ear.

Kate looked deep into the Major's eyes. "Who are you?" "Major Zalar, Ma'am!"

"General Zalar did not have a son."

Major Zalar looked at Miles and snarled, then knocked him down with a gun butt.

"No! No! No!" Kate cried as she pounded the Major with her fists.

The Major Morphed to Malcolm and shoved her to the floor. "I want those codes now?"

"Why, Malcolm? Is there not enough destruction out there already?"

"There is a silence in heaven that my thunder will break!"

"What?"

"Our Father who art in heaven!" Miles mumbled a prayer.

A ZZ Goon started to fire at him.

"No! No? No!" Kate ran to his side.

"That prayer is forbidden in this holy place!" Malcolm snarled.

"He won't do it again, okay?" Kate stood in front of Miles.

"No matter. Give me those codes, or he will die a slow, agonizing death." "Don't give them to him, Madam President. Please?" Miles pleaded. "Thy Kingdom come. Thy…"

"Shut up!" Malcolm waved his hand, and a gate opened in a nearby wall. Over the gate is written "*Lasciate ogne speranza, voi ch'intrate.*" Just inside the gate were: a roaring lion, a snarling leopard, and a rabid wolf.

Two ZZ Goons shoved Miles through the gate and the beasts loped toward Miles with teeth bared.

Malcolm held up his hand, and the beasts paused. "If he reaches Acheron and crosses, there is no coming back."

"Madame President! Don't worry. It's a deception. Charon will not let me pass! Thy will be…" Miles said just before a swarm of hornets and wasps began to sting him so severely, he began to cry out in agony.

Kate hesitated and turned away as maggots began to eat at Miles's and crawl up his legs."

"Stop! You are so damned powerful; why not kill me and just take the codes."

"You know it's tuned to your biorhythms and is deactivated if you are forced and dies with you if you are killed," Malcolm said.

There was a loud rumble, and the floor shook beneath their feet.

Malcolm looked scared for a moment.

Kate picked up on it. "What are you so afraid of?"

"I fear nothing!" Malcolm flinched as another loud rumble was heard, and the ground shook.

Kate smirked at him. "My, God! You are afraid!"

"The codes! Now!"

"No, Madame President! He hopes to upset God's timetable." Miles pleaded.

Malcolm waved his hand, and Miles was covered in festering boils. He dropped to his knees in agony.

"Stop! Ok! We are all going to die anyway." Kate said.

Malcolm grinned. "Yes, but not in his time. In my time!" He stopped to swell with pride.

"No! No!" Miles mumbled as pain made him fall into a fetal position, his face contorted in agony.

Kate held out her arm. "Release him, and I'll give you the codes."

"No! The codes first."

Kate looked at the agony on Mile's face and nodded. She held out her arm, and a Robo Techie began to scan her arm with a microchip scanner. One by one, the codes appeared on a monitor.

Kate was forced to be seated at a keyboard.

Malcolm scowled, and she began to type in her passwords.

As they appeared, Malcolm keyed in the launch code.

Kate looked at Miles in agony. "Release him now!"

Malcolm waved his hand, and Miles tumbled from the gate, and the gate closed.

Miles was weak but got to his feet. He looked at Kate and shook his head.

Kate winked.

Miles looked puzzled.

Malcolm was gleeful as the monitors revealed the missile silo doors were opening, and the missiles ready to launch. "I will have a throne here before Yahweh does! My will be done!" Malcolm roared, then looked worried as the Silo doors started to close. He turned and glared at Kate, then growled. "What are you doing?"

"I have done all you asked." Kate snapped.

Before Malcolm could answer, Oskar ran up beside Malcolm and pointed to a BVR monitor that showed Sam inside the Temple standing beside John.

"I am sorry he got by security somehow." Oskar chortled.

"Good." Malcolm seemed pleased.

"I will take care of it, Master!"

"You are to do nothing."

Oskar looked puzzled. "He got past the Nephilim, but I can stop him."

Malcolm knocked Oskar down with an invisible fist. "You stand no chance against Michael!" Malcolm gritted his teeth before he relaxed and smiled. "He can only help Sam so much before he is in rebellion. Maybe soon I will have company in hell!" Malcolm hurried out of the room.

Once he was gone, a wall of mud began to surround Kate and Miles. It was soon filled with straw and dried to form bricks, then began to close in around them.

Kate looked up to see three einsatz gruppe ZZ Goons drawing their weapons. She put her arm around Miles, and he held on to her. Kate was determined to face bravely what so many of her people had faced so many years ago.

Oskar motioned to his ZZ Goons men to backoff and let Miles and Kate be killed by the wall now looming over and inches from crushing them.

Miles looked on in horror as Kate touched the micro-chip implant on her right arm and tapped in Morse Code taps. He was rusty on his Morse Code but did understand that part of the message said, "Activate!"

Miles pushed Kate's finger away from the chip and glowed at her. "You have not only betrayed me but all humans! How could you?"

"Let's pray."

"It's a little late for that."

"Please trust that I have not done what you think I have."

"I don't know what to think."

"You believe in angels?"

"Yes."

"Please just repeat this prayer after me."

"We already said the Lord's prayer."

"Yes. But this is for John and his Keepers."

"We need to hurry and escape."

"Past those goons and through those thick walls?"

"How about Joshua?"

"The myth of Jericho?"

"It's okay. I will pray alone." Kate paused, then began. "O glorious Archangel Michael, Prince of the heavenly host, defend The Keepers of The Word and us in the struggle against the Anti-Christ! Bring forth The Sword of The word and strike down these walls."

Miles added a half-hearted "Amen!"

Oskar and his ZZ Goons covered their ears so as not to hear the prayer. It so angered them they decided to shoot Kate and Miles. They aimed to fire at Kate and Miles. Just before they did, their guns were stuck from their hands by an unseen force and the walls came tumbling down.

CHAPTER TWENTY-FOUR

John was kneeling before Michelangelo's painting of The Creation of Adam but with Malcolm's smiling face replacing God. He mumbled prayers as unintelligible as pain from The Chip would allow. "Welcome, Sam. I'm glad you could join us." John smiled as Sam approached him.

"No! I came to free you!" Sam pulled the Clovis knife from his belt.

"No, Sam! Please! "John held up his hands and backed away.

The Keepers who were mumbling prayers to Malcolm stopped praying. A few got up and advanced toward Sam.

Sam grabbed John's right arm by the wrist and jabbed the Clovis knife into the site of the implant on John's right hand. A dozen Keepers were close to descending on him when Sam dislodged The Chip with the Clovis knifepoint. The Chip fell to the floor, and Sam crushed it with his foot.

"You have killed me, Sam? Why?" John fell to his knees and keeled over.

Two Keepers began to swing their fists at Sam. One picked up a bronze candlestick holder from the altar and was about to hit Sam with it.

"No! No! Stop!" John yelled as he got to his feet.

The Keepers backed off.

John looked at the smashed chip, then at Sam. "Thank you." He gazed at the Clovis knife and smiled.

"How do you feel?"

"As if my soul has returned. Bless you, Sam." John smiled and nodded before he turned and looked out over his flock. "What about all of them?"

"I hope I can get to the servo room and stop the transmissions. You use your skill to keep them here."

"I will try. But Sam, there is a legion of Facistas and einsatz gruppe ZZ Goons guarding that room. And…" John paused to look frightened.

"And what?"

"And Ty is held captive to be killed the moment you enter."

Before Sam could reply, a Laser Blast whizzed by Sam's head and blew the painting of Adam off the Temple wall. He looked toward the back of the Temple and saw a dozen Facistas coming with machetes raised. They were followed by a dozen ZZ einsatz gruppe goons firing lasers.

John and The Keepers ducked for cover.

Sam stood tall as Laser Blasts hit all around him. There was not a hint of fear in him as he put the Clovis knife away and loaded his bow with a rosewood arrow. He drew the bowstring back and let the arrow fly. The Obsidian arrow point tore through one Facista and passed on through two more behind him. All of them fell hard to the ground. He reloaded his bow and quickly fired arrows that began dropping the ZZ goons.

"You surely have put on the armor of God." John looked on in amazement.

Sam did not reply as he was busy losing a volley of arrows downing every Facista and ZZ goon that drew close. He was down to his last arrow when Malcolm appeared twenty yards away. Sam felt a rush of excitement as he drew down on Malcolm and let the arrow fly.

The arrow was inches from Malcolm's heart when Malcolm grabbed it in mid-air, then broke it in half.

Sam dropped the bow and pulled out the Clovis knife. "Come on, Malcolm! Let's finish it!'

"Sam! We've tried that already. But okay." Malcolm stepped up beside Sam and puffed up his chest.

Sam started to plunge the knife into Malcolm's chest but hesitated when Tiye entered and stood beside Malcolm.

A squad of einsatz gruppe ZZ Goons surrounded Sam as he and Tiye stared at each other. They pointed their guns to fire but Malcolm waved them off.

Sam put the Clovis knife away, looked Tiye over, and shook his head at Malcolm. "Is this the latest model, Tiye, Malcolm?"

"Nope, the real thing." Malcolm put his arm around her.

Tiye seemed to welcome it.

Sam looked hard at her right hand, and there was not even the slightest trace of an implant. It hurt him to the depths of his soul that she had truly betrayed him. He raised the Clovis knife and lunged at her. A ZZ Goon whacked Sam with a gun butt, and Sam fell to the floor. Two other ZZ Goons held him down.

"I bring you a new member of your flock, John. Maybe you should give him last rites." Malcolm looked down on Sam, then morphed to his best Christ-like visage and filled the Tabernacle with soft lights and pleasing aromas. He reached out to the last of John's flock gathered before him with his arms. "My good people, all I ask is fairness. Have I not fed and clothed you well? Have I not indulged your every desire? The world outside is doomed, yet I have given you a haven." Malcolm paused to look humble with misty eyes. "All I ask is that you bow down in thanks to me for all the gifts you have received. Let us pray – to me!"

The flock was crippled by pain from megaIPI's. Some were forced to their knees, but some endured the agony and found the strength not to kneel.

"Turn up the Pain!" Malcolm turned to Oskar.

"It is at peak Amps now, Master. For some reason, the signal is weak."

Malcolm looked at Tiye.

"All systems were working perfectly last time I checked." Tiye insisted.

Malcolm was not so sure. "Make them sing to me."

Oskar hit a control button, and The Keepers began to sing. "Rock of ages cleft for me. Let me hide myself in thee…."

"No! No! No! Stop it!" Malcolm covered his ears.

Oskar hit the controls several times, but The Keepers kept singing.

Sam shook off his wooziness and looked up at Malcolm. "Not a good time to pass the collection plate, eh, Malcolm?"

Malcolm looked at Tiye. "What is going on?"

"I don't know. When I left the Control Room, everything was at full power." Tiye replied.

Malcolm gazed at her with doubt before he turned to Oskar. "Get to the Control Room and boost the signal. I need them on their knees!"

John stepped up and turned to the keepers. "We must keep the faith, my people. Please pray with me." He bowed his head and folded his hands in prayer. "The Lord is my shepherd he maketh…"

Malcolm exploded with rage as he morphed into the Red Dragon. As he did, the ground shook, and the Tabernacle began to fill with fire. In the chaos of the fire and falling debris, Sam spied a small opening that the quake had formed. He looked at Tiye and motioned toward it. She shook her head and backed off. Sam started to grab her and pull her along, but she disappeared into the smoke. He hesitated then turned and ran to the opening.

When he had passed through it, he found himself in long polished marble passageways that were lined with huge storage bins of foodstuffs. There were giant freezers and storage silos as far as he could see freshwater pouring from deep mountain springs filled huge vats. Sam paused to taste it and marveled at its cool refreshing taste. He heard the jackboots of the ZZ Goons and broke into a run. He was at full speed when he rounded a corner too fast, slipped, and fell down a chasm in the rock. He tumbled into the darkness until he came to a stop outside the cavern. When he had a chance to look around, Sam found himself alone, standing in the shadows of Cathedral Spires.

As he looked up at them, t here was a pale sun behind the broken crosses on top of the Spires, now completely formed into Gothic Cathedral facades. They cast their unholy swastika shadow on where Sam stood. As he stood in the swastika shadow, he felt a chill to his bones and the insidious creep of evil into his soul. He tried to move but his legs would not obey.

Sam closed his eyes, gripped the Golden Acorn, and prayed for the strength to break free. When he opened them, he found he was standing in what was left of Mariposa Grove. Where once there had been hundreds of majestic Giant Sequoias, there now stood only the Three Graces and, some distance away, The Grizzly Giant, the oldest tree in the world.

Sam stood in awe of their majesty and watched as the noonday sun caused The Three Graces to cast a shadow pointing to the base of The Grizzly Giant. Sam felt compelled to follow the shadow until he stood in the sunlight at the base of the Grizzly Giant.

As Sam watched, the huge tree branches seemed to reach the sky and part the heavens. Its branches were laden with ripe fruits, and as he watched, they morphed to acorns that fell as rain, some pelting him until he went to his knees and bowed his head. When the pelting stopped, he looked up to see The Great Grizzly Tree faded into a mist, and Golden Gates appeared in front of him. He was struck weak with awe when he looked past the gates to see a bare stone altar on a book with seven seals.

Sam slowly got to his knees and began to move toward the altar. He stopped when he heard a familiar voice.

"Hello, Sam." Tiye's voice broke into his thoughts. "Looks like you found it.

Sam turned to see her flanked by Facistas and a Squad of einsatz gruppe ZZ Goons. His first instinct was to deck her. He balled his fists, but The Black Dog was dead. "More tricks, Malcolm?"

"No, it's the real me." Tiye insisted.

Sam grabbed her by the arms and shook her. "Where is the real, Ty?"

Tiye looked fearful until she broke his hold. "Back off, Sam, if you care about John and his followers."

"What if I don't?"

"They will be slaughtered unless we do as Malcolm wants."

"He's going to do that anyway!"

"No! We have sort of a deal."

"I know you do!" Sam snorted in discontent.

"Think what you will. My way, many have a chance to live." Tiye started to move toward the altar.

Sam reached out to stop her, but two ZZ einsatz gruppe Goons held him back while the Facistas blocked his path.

"No, Ty? No! I can't let you touch that book!" Sam tried to get past the Facistas and Goons, but they restrained him.

Tiye looked back and smiled. "Oh, but I must!" Tiye retorted as she went through the Golden Gates.

Malcolm chuckled with delight as he watched Tiye and Sam on a monitor. He turned to look out on The Keepers, who were now on their knees as John, who had been newly implanted, led The Keepers in singing Malcolm's praises.

Oskar Direwanger, Konrads Kalejs, Oskar Bach-Zelewski, and a host of his best Demons were at his side. He glanced at the doomsday clock. It read: 11:59:59. "Hurry, woman! Hurry!" Malcolm mumbled as he watched Tiye head to the altar, then turn to watch the monitors of the missile silos. The silo doors were opening, and soon they would be flying. "Soon, Michael! Your Judgment Day is coming soon! Yes! Very soon now!"

Sam watched in horror as the Golden Gates started to close.

He struggled to free himself from the grip of the ZZ Goons. They seemed to enjoy the futility of his struggle until he got one arm free and withdrew the bone whistle from a pocket. As Sam put the whistle to his mouth, the ZZ Goons slapped at his hands, and the Facistas raised their machetes to strike at him. Sam wondered if he was too late when he blew the whistle with hope and a prayer.

Moments later, Tenaya appeared in warrior's dress on his Cayuse pony, followed by a dozen young warriors. The Warriors loosed volleys of holy arrows that tore the human mask from the ZZ Goons and Facistas revealing their Demon self before they tumbled through a portal into a hell full of the hungry maws of Harpies. Then the

Ahwahnechee warriors rode off across the valley yelling whoops of victory.

After they were gone, Sam ran as hard as he could and barely made it inside before the Golden Gates closed behind him. Once inside, Sam was awed by the beauty of the vault containing The Book of Life. It was lined with finely polished marble that was pleasing to the eye. There was soft light but no visible source, and deep in your soul, you knew you were in a holy place. He paused for a moment of reverence, then looked up to see Tiye approaching the altar holding the book with seven seals.

He did not see any Ahwahnechee Cherubim's, and that made him suspicious.

As Tiye moved slowly toward the altar, an earth tremor almost knocked her off her feet. When she got back up, she wondered if she should still proceed. She did not wonder long as an unseen hand seemed to shove her along. She was almost at the altar when Sam appeared, running toward her. She stopped, turned around, and glared at him.

"Sam? What are you…where did you come from?"

"Never mind. Just stop!"

"You don't understand, Sam."

Sam grabbed her arm to pull her away from the altar.

Tiye did not resist. "Go ahead. But if you don't stand aside, he will win!"

"No! If you touch that book! He will win!"

Tiye ran past Sam to the altar and broke open the seals of the book!

"No! No! No!" Sam ran after her.

It was too late she had opened the book.

Sam looked scared, then dumbfounded. He waited for heavenly vengeance that never came. He watched as Tiye flipped through the pages of the book.

They were blank.

"What? What's going on, Tiye?"

Tiye gave him a look of disgust, then mellowed some. "You ruined it!"

"What? I..." Sam studied her face as the Hologram began to fade – then he smiled with admiration.

The Red Dragon roared with rage. His first impulse was to destroy Tiye and Sam in a brutal and long-lasting way. He held back because he thought Michael was involved, so he would wait until Michael was exposed. Then he would end it one way or the other. It was hard to contain his rage and wait. The great deceiver despised deception, especially from a woman he had loved before the dawn of creation. Malcolm's hurt ran so deep he almost made his move. He stopped and felt a wisp of fear as he thought he heard the distant sound of a trumpet.

Cowering in fear nearby, Ilse, Eric, and Oskar whispered to each other as they huddled together and watched megaBVR Monitors from a far corner of the room.

"Are you going to tell him?" Eric asked Oskar.

Oskar managed a crooked smile as he shook his head.

Eric trembled and eased into the shadows. "When he finds out, it will be the Harpies for us, again!"

"Yes, but we will have had our taste of revenge." Oskar chortled.

Ilse had contempt for them both. "You were both supposed to watch her. You lusted for her instead!"

Neither Oskar nor Eric responded until Malcolm got in their face, "What are you mumbling about. Is there something I need to know?"

"No! No! Nothing, Master!" They said in unison.

Malcolm turned his gaze on Ilse, then booted up a nearby monitor. It read: "IMP- OMEGA- VAR.CHIP 666-Tiye Abramson-status- Active." He sighed in relief, then turned and glared at all his Demons. "Good. The missiles are on their way."

"Yes, Master, but has the unworthy touched the holy of holies?"

"Not yet." Malcolm grinned.

"I saw her on the monitor..." Ilse offered.

"You saw what she wanted us to see. Now make sure no one gets into the server room or there will be no end to the agony I prepare for you."

Ilse started to say something. Oskar and Eric stared her down.

Malcolm looked worried as he thought he saw a flicker in the feed to the monitors. "You are sure this feed is live?"

"Yes, Master. Is something wrong?" Oskar asked.

"I sense deception."

"Who would dare deceive you?" Eric wondered barely holding concealing his fear.

"If there is deception it is not my doing, Master!" Ilse spoke up."

Malcolm looked past her and gave Oskar and Eric a withering stare. "You guarded Lillith well, did you not?"

"Yes, Master!" Oskar and Eric muttered in unison.

Ilse scoffed.

"Go bring Lillith to me."

"Is she not in the tabernacle with the book of life?" Oskar offered.

"A holographic lie only she could project." Malcolm looked suspicious. "Go now and bring her to me!"

Oskar, Ilse, and Eric looked at each other and began to back away in fear.

"Go now! And have John Pottos begin a sermon of praise to me!" Malcolm looked at his J-Day clock.

It read: 00:00:10

Oskar and Eric sneaked a look at a small secret monitor. It showed the missiles self-destructing and splashing harmlessly into the sea.

"What if he finds out?" Eric whispered to Oskar.

"We will suffer no more than we have, and we will have had our revenge." Oskar insisted,

"Asmodeus help us!"

They quickly turned the small monitor off, then looked pale with fear.

Malcolm glared at them. "What? Is something wrong?"

"No, Master!" Eric and Oskar said together.

"Yes, Master. They have betrayed you!' Ilse spoke up.

Eric and Oskar looked scared as they each expected the other to answer. "No, Master. She lies. We have done as you willed!"

Ilse looked at them with contempt.

"Ilse speaks the truth." Malcolm grinned a sardonic grin.

"Yes, Master. I tried to stop them." Ilse stepped away from Oskar and Eric.

"What would you have us do, Master?" Oskar and Eric pleaded.

"Go to hell!" Malcolm growled as he morphed to The Red Dragon and roared before he cast Oskar and Eric down into the maws of hungry Harpies.

Ilse watched and smiled until she began to descend also. "No, Master. I did not betray you."

"You did not stop them." Malcolm waved Ilse into hell and closed the portal.

Once he was alone, Malcolm looked at a monitor showing Mt. Tambora rumbling loud and threatening to erupt. He smiled as a missile appeared to hit it.

Moments later, it erupted, destroying the Sundra Islands and all of Indonesia. The eruption was so loud it could be heard 3000 miles away and caused a chain reaction resulting in Indonesia's 400 other volcanoes erupting. The explosions caused Giant Tsunamis to send huge waves toward Australia and the Philippines. The South China Sea was a bubbling cauldron, and any shipping upon it was obliterated. The fabled "Ring of Fire" that included the Southern, Northern, and part of the Eastern Hemispheres, which had slept for hundreds of years, lived up to its name and sent fire, poison smoke, and deadly ash across one-seventh of the world's population.

Bits of ash fell on the pristine snow of the Antarctic.

The Red Dragon watched through a glass darkly at monitors and smiled at the code names he had for the seven Super Volcanoes: Ephesus, Smyrna, Pergamos, Thyatira, Sardis, Philadelphia, and Laodicea. Their real names were Yellowstone, Lake Toba in Sumatra, Aira in Japan, Long Valley in California, Taupo in New Zealand, and Valles in northern Mexico. They were all spewing steam in pre-eruption amounts. Soon the missiles would hit them, and the earth would be a burned-out cinder.

Or so it seemed on all the main monitors which he knew was a deception programmed by Kaye and Tiye – as was Tiye's breaking of the seals. He turned off the monitor and grinned a sardonic grin before he went to a CHIP monitor and began to program his revenge.

Kate looked at her watch, which had a Mini-HDR-COMM.

She smiled when she saw a flashing red light. "The missiles have been deactivated?"

Miles looked doubtful.

"Launch codes needed in-flight verification. A backup fail-safe, few knew about." Kate smiled.

"But I saw you punch in "activate."

"Yes, so all would not know it was the complete opposite signal."

"Oh? So, he didn't get those?"

"No! I couldn't tell you earlier."

"What will he do now?"

"Most probably come for us. I'm sorry." Kate looked sad.

"It's Okay. I'm glad you did it."

"I had little choice."

"I'm sorry I said those things to you."

"Forget it."

They felt a tremor and heard a rumble, looked at each other. with respect, then held hands.

"What now?" Miles wondered.

"Please come join us in prayer?" John's voice broke into their thoughts.

They looked up at a BVR monitor and saw John standing at the pulpit in Satan's Temple.

"John? Thank God." Kate looked puzzled. "But how?" "Well, let's give thanks to Tiye Abrams and her electronic wizardry. Then let's pray for her, Sam, and the God-fearing few that remain in this world."

Kate and Miles nodded, then knelt and folded their hands in prayer. As they did, they could smell the scent of brimstone and feel the heat of the hellfire coming their way.

CHAPTER TWENTY-FIVE

Tiye and Sam stood quietly by Tiye's Holographic altar, which had almost completely vanished.

Sam had to smile in admiration "So, none of this was real?"

"Of course not! Why didn't you let it playout?" Tiye grumped.

"I didn't..."

"Yes, you did. You ruined the deception because you never trusted me."

"I..."

"You think I'd ever let him find the real thing."

"Is there such a...thing?"

"God only knows." Tiye thought it over. "But he is certain it is here somewhere?" She gave Sam a quizzical look.

"Why are you looking at me like that?" Sam backed off a little.

"He keeps insisting you know where it is."

Sam gripped the Golden Acorn and shook his head. "For a lowly outcast Indian boy, I sure get a lot of celestial attention."

"Mostly holograms." Tiye looked apologetic. "Some I sent. I'm sorry."

"Right! So, what's your next move, Madam Wizard?"

"We wait on his vengeance." Tiye grimaced.

"Would he harm his queen?" Sam needled.

"Don't go there, Sam."

"That's the real question, isn't it?"

"What?"

"Where do we go now?"

Tiye slumped and looked a little frightened. "I have to go back."

"No, you don't. We can take our chances at Pywiack!"

Tiye smiled at him before she looked serious. She touched the Golden Acorn and looked deep into his eyes. "Not all that has happened to you can be explained by holograms. Perhaps Tenaya protects you here." She sighed. "But my only chance to survive is to beg his forgiveness and become his Queen."

"No! No, please. At least come with to Pywiack and see that maybe Tenaya will protect us both."

"A nice dream, Sam. But the best chance for us both is for me to go back and see what I can do there."

Sam drew close. He raised his fingertips and waited for her's to touch his. Tiye smiled and touched his fingertips. Their eyes met with tender understanding, and they shared a long moment of perfect love.

Sam broke the touch and slumped. "I never felt so good and so bad at the same time in my life."

"I think you are suffering from quest withdrawal."

"I know…it was a stupid quest from the get-go." Sam laughed at himself. "A man who believes in nothing should never believe in anything."

"I don't think you are as cynical as you pretend. Besides, It isn't over yet."

Sam looked serious. "What do you think he will pull next?"

"He will come with such cunning we may not be able to see through it."

"How will we deal with it?"

"You go to Pywiack and call on the Tenaya angels. I will go to the Temple and hope."

Tiye said with a little shiver.

"Is it possible he'll just forgive and forget?"

"No. The book of Revelations says he has a date with God. All this is to try to avoid that." "The book of Revelations is nuts as the man who wrote it!

It's so convoluted no one can, say what it means." "Watch it, Sam. You don't mock God's word."

"So, you understand all that obscure imagery and confusing prophecy?"

"Few people understand it all. But I don't question it."

"When did you get religion?"

Tiye had to think it over. "I think when I was 12 at my Bat Mitzvah."

"You could have fooled me."

"It was always there, Sam. As it is with you."

"If you mean the Great Spirit, I agree. I have done as my ancestor wanted and fought to protect the book – even though it wasn't for real."

"I'm glad to see you finally believed in something."

Sam looked hurt for a long moment. "I wanted to believe. Ahwahnee would return to its former glory." He stopped and looked sad. "Your Holocasts had me believing that might be possible but as with all such things, it wasn't real."

Tiye took his hand and drew close. "I can program us an Ahwahnee that will be so real you won't be able to tell it isn't!" Tiye touched his fingertips to hers.

Sam smiled with immense joy when he felt the tingle of true love. "Yeah! Why not? It's all in mind anyway." Sam put his arms around her, and they shared a sweet kiss.

Tiye broke the kiss and stepped back.

"What's going on, Tiye?"

"What if there is a real Book of Life somewhere in Yosemite?"

Sam paused and looked around. "I thought we agreed that was all myth."

"What if this wasn't Eden, Sam?"

"It was to my people."

"East of Eden?"

"What?"

"Nod? Where the Eden outcasts were sent. What if they took the book with them."

"I suppose anything in myth anything is possible…"

"…and The sons of God knew the daughters of men…"

"I always thought that was a strange verse."

"If they came here with the book, the Ahwahnechee were tasked with guarding it."

"Come on, Tiye…"

"What would be more natural than protecting it with a majestic oak?"

"It would take some acorn to grow a tree like that!" Sam chided.

Tiye touched the Golden Acorn on Sam's necklace. "Just a trinket, right?"

Sam put his hand over hers and they both felt at peace for a long moment. When they took their hands away, they looked at each other for answers.

"It's not all cyber tricks and BVR holograms, Sam. Ahwahnee is a magic place."

Sam sighed agreement. "You don't really think such a book exists here?"

Tiye looked worried. "Maybe…maybe not. But if he finds it, all bets are off."

"Come on. It can't be anywhere around here and if he projects one, we will ignore it!"

"Sam, there are a lot of things going on holographic projections don't explain."

"What are you saying?"

"It was no hologram that saved you from your fall."

"What?"

"I checked every log and there were no holograms sent." Tiye paused and gave him a serious look. "You did jump right?"

Sam nodded slowly and looked doubtful. "You sure?"

"Yes, it's…" Tiye dropped to her knees in agony.

"Tiye? What is it?" Sam tried to comfort her.

"I thought I muted his IPI projectors…but they are back and… Oh God, Sam, it hurts so bad." Tiye fell over into the fetal position.

Sam pulled the Clovis knife, picked up her right hand, and did not see any implant site. "I can't find the implant. Where is it?"

Before Tiye could reply, the hologram faded, and they were outside on the ground, deep in the shadows of Cathedral spires where Malcolm appeared in a Holocast. "Tiye will die in agony unless you lead me to the real altar and The Book of Life." Malcolm thundered.

Sam looked at Tiye folded up in agony. "Stop it! Leave her alone! It was her hologram. There is no tree or book here. You won't gain anything by her death!"

"I will gain the heavens and the earth if you will only do as I command."

Sam could not bear to watch Tiye's agony. He paused and thought it over. "Tenaya, I pray you to protect this woman as if she were my bride!" Sam said as he removed the necklace from around his neck. He knelt beside her and started to put it around Tiye's neck.

As he did, he dropped it to the ground.

Before he could pick it up, the Golden Acorn sprouted and began to grow into a majestic Black Oak Tree laden with ripe fruit, resembling apples. Moments later, the Black Oak morphed into a stand of Lebanese Cedar. As they watched in awe, a Phoenician-style Temple began to appear before them. It seemed to have a large outer room, but they were in a smaller room, only 20 feet long and 30 feet high. The floor was of the finest marble floor, and the walls were in a wainscoted pattern which was overlaid by gold which also overlaid the walls and ceiling. There were no windows, but many ceramic lamps filled with olive oil and flax wicks to provide humble lighting.

On the cella was an altar made of acacia wood and overlaid with bronze. It had four ram horns projected from the top four corners, and a bronze grating covered a sacrificial fire. Behind the altar were two 20-foot-high olive-wood angels with wingspans of 10 feet that touched the tips.

Before them they saw four fearsome beasts that blocked their path; A lamb with seven horns and seven eyes, a great red dragon with seven heads and ten horns, a leopard with seven heads and ten horns and a lamb with two horns that spoke like a dragon.

"Your projection?" Sam looked at Tiye and backed off.

Tiye shook her head and watched the beasts bear down on Sam. They were about to tear him apart when she dropped to her knees and folded her hands in prayer. "Oh God, I come to you as Enoch. I lift my hands unto thee. Be it unto me as it pleases you. I require nothing but thee, and through thee, and for thy honor and glory. I hope I shall be satisfied and shall not die until you gather the clouds together and judge all things. When in a moment I shall be changed and dwell with thee forever."

Sam was about to run when the beasts disappeared. He looked up, smiled at Tiye, and sighed hard in relief.

They turned and looked toward the altar to see, standing behind the altar was a man dressed in a prophet's robes. At his side were two Lions, who lay down beside two lambs. Behind him, seven Ahwahnechee Angels were holding seven trumpets and were bathed from behind in celestial light. A light brighter than the sun that did not hurt their eyes or cause a single blink.

"Why are you here?" The Prophet demanded.

Tiye tried to back away, but the pain made her reach for the book. Sam pulled her away from the altar, and she folded in pain?

"She is in great pain. Are you an angel? Can you help her?"

"I am Daniel. He who shut and sealed the book until the time of the end. Let she who is of the blood break the last seal!" Daniel intoned. His voice was pleasant but commanding.

Tiye grimaced in pain and started to reach for the seal. "Sam, I hurt so much. Let me touch it and take the pain away!"

"Are you Ahwahnechee?" Daniel asked Sam.

"No...I..."Sam started to turn and walk away,

"Why have you abandoned your guardianship?" Daniel roared at Sam.

"I am not..."

"Are you of people chosen to be The Guardians of the book?" A celestial light focused on the Red Seal, which seemed to be made of wax and had seven stars embossed on it.

Sam felt a pain in his right hand. He looked at his palm, and there were seven stars. He felt a surge of regret so powerful he thought he would die. He turned back and spoke with newfound pride. "Yes! Yes, I am Ahwahnechee."

Tiye's fingers were inches from touching the seal when Sam pulled them back and blocked her path to the altar. He swelled with pride as he stood tall ready to give his life to stop anyone from touching the book.

Daniel smiled.

"Open the seal, Sam. Or she will die an agonizing death." The Red Dragon roared from a Hologram.

"Do not fear him. He may not enter the Holy of Holies." Daniel spoke.

"Do not listen to Daniel! He is a seer, but not a Prophet!

Open the book and save the world. Open it, or she will die, Sam!" The Red Dragon snarled.

Tiye fell back in agony. She looked up at Sam for help with pleading eyes as her body contorted in pain – then she fell lifeless.

Sam looked up at Daniel. "Please help her. She is infected with evil that is beyond prayer."

"You are a guardian. You have the means to save her. It has been with you from the beginning. Take care of her, for this is a woman in favor with God." Daniel faded.

"Please! I…don't go…help me!" Sam had tears in his eyes as he looked down at the lifeless Tiye. He held the clovis knife and knew if he could cut out the implant, she might live. Quickly, he examined both her hands and arms and could find no hint of an implant. No matter how carefully they implanted, they always left a small trace of a scar.

Sam could find none.

Then he remembered a passage from Genesis. It was something about God putting enmity between Satan and the woman. Satan would bruise her head, and she would bruise his heel. Sam ran his finger through her hair but stopped and smiled – knowing Satan's perverted mind. He reached down, took off her shoes, and examined both her heels.

Sam sighed in relief when he saw the small implant scar on her right heel. He calmed himself until his hand was steady, and then he cut the implant out.

When it hit the incense in the air, it vaporized.

Tiye did not respond, so he lifted her up in his arms and kissed her with a tender kiss of hope, followed by a breath of life.

She did not respond, and he almost despaired.

Then he felt her fingertips touch his. The touch sent shivers of joy through his being, and he rejoiced to the depths of his soul when she opened her eyes and looked up at him.

"Are you still in pain?" Sam asked as he slowly eased her down on her feet.

"Only my ankle." Tiye smiled. "How did you know?"

"Hey, I'm an Ahwahnechee Guardian. Can't give away all our secrets!"

Tiye fell into his arms, and they shared a long hug of relief before she stepped back and looked around to see The Book of Life was on the altar, but none of the seals were broken. "We don't belong here, Sam."

"I know. And we must never tell of it."

Suddenly, the room went dark. They held onto each other.

until the shaking stopped. Once it had, they were in the shadow of Cathedral Spires.

Standing before them was The Red Dragon. He glared at them with his Demon eyes lighting up the darkness before he morphed to his most handsome self and pointed his finger at Tiye. "I bow to one who is even a greater deceiver than I, Sam. Beware of the Delilah who claims to love you. She is a harlot who betrayed us both."

"Enough, Malcolm. No one believes you anymore," Sam insisted.

"Ask her to tell you the truth."

"Truth? How would you know anything about that?" Sam looked at Tiye. She frowned, then glared at Malcolm.

"Have her swear before Yahweh that she is not Lillith, the Queen of Demons who became the snake that tempted Eve out of jealousy because Adam spurned her!"

"Don't you ever get tired of lies? And don't you have better things to do like getting fitted for an asbestos suit?" Sam needled.

"Look upon this, Sam." Malcolm conjured a megaBVR projection showing him and Tiye in his bedroom, close by his bed, holding hands and drawing close to kiss.

"You come of your own free will?" Malcolm asked.

"Yes." Tiye smiled.

"And what of Sam?"

"Sam is insane. So, I choose you if you will have me."

"Will you open the book?"

"Yes, to save us both."

"It must be defiled, so chaos fills the heavens."

"What of, Sam?"

"He will believe you have been implanted and help you to find the way."

"You are sure the implant is a fake?"

"Yes. But you must put on a convincing performance that you are in great pain from the evil old me?"

They chuckled together.

Malcolm morphed to Donavan and drew her close. They shared a quick kiss. "That brings back memories of long, long ago."

"Can we forget the past and concentrate on our future." Tiye cooed.

"Yes. We will have our garden again, devoid of the sons of God and the daughters of men."

"I know." Tiye pulled him close. "So, let's not waste any time we have!"

Malcolm smiled; he took her face in his hands and gently pulled it to his for a kiss. The kiss was not quick or forced but passionate and long.

Tiye broke the kiss and fell back on the bed with her arms and legs open in an inviting pose.

Sam had to look away. "I don't care to see any more of your photo-shopped porno, Malcolm."

"Okay. Ask her if any of that is a lie?"

Sam looked at Tiye and waited for her to say something.

Tiye did not respond.

"See! She does not answer because she knows the truth. She is truly Lillith, and her Demon spirit is in every woman who has betrayed a Lover, a Captain, or a Kingdom."

Sam stared hard at Tiye, waiting for an answer.

"What can I say, Sam?"

"A simple denial would help." Sam seemed a little worried.

"No! You either believe him or trust me!" Tiye turned and started to walk away.

Satan smiled.

"I...I want to believe you. Wait! Stop!" Sam called after her." Tiye kept on walking until she disappeared deep into the swastika shadow of Cathedral Spires.

Sam started to run after her. He stopped and turned to see a grin on Malcolm's face. He called for The Black Dog to tear into Malcolm's smug face. It did not respond. Instead, he felt a strange sense of melancholy.

"Go after her, Sam! She deserves to die for her betrayal!" Malcolm prodded as he moved to the tip of the Shadow of a Cathedral Spire and stood in the dark circle formed by a shadow of a broken cross swastika. "If she is what you say she is, has she not been true to her nature?" Sam asked.

"What? Have you gone soft? Where is your fierce anger?"

Sam shook his head. "I don't know."

"You can't let her do that to you and live! Hurry! Go after her now! Kill!"

"No!"

"Why not?"

"Because that is what you want!"

"Sam, you must seek vengeance for your peace of mind." "In love is forgiveness."

"No! Not, Sam Rathe! Have you gone the way of the meek John and The Keepers?"

"Perhaps I have. For it is they that will inherit the earth in God's coming world."

"Don't say that! Don't ever say that to me!" Malcolm fumed, then morphed into The Red Dragon. He roared in anger and breathed fire that did not burn, then turned his wrath on Sam.

Sam backed away, then stopped as he suddenly felt full of The Great Spirit. It was not the raging anger of The Black Dog but a feeling of quiet strength. He stood tall and looked The Red Dragon in the eyes. "I am Ahwahnechee of the ancient Ahwahnee guardians. This is Ahwahnee. I want you and your evil gone from here!"

"You think you are done with me, Sam? No! You are mine. You will surely die now!" The Red Dragon snapped.

Sam grinned and pulled the bone whistle from his pocket.

"Is that supposed to frighten me?" Malcolm scoffed.

Sam sensed fear as Malcolm backed away. "It's just a dime- store trinket, right?"

Malcolm grinned and nodded.

"Unless I have faith. Then it is more than that." Sam closed his eyes, said a silent prayer, and started to blow the whistle.

"No! Put that away!" The Red Dragon roared, then flew into a rage.

Sam shook his head and blew the whistle. Seconds later, seven Ahwahnechee Angels blew their seven trumpets. The sound of the trumpets echoed with a roar of thunder, and the world shook.

Sam was forced to his knees. When he looked up, he saw Michael, The Archangel standing with the Ahwahnechee Angels at his side. With a swipe of his hand, he sent the fire away.

The Red Dragon turned his rage toward Michael. "You don't belong here!"

"Not yet!"

"This is my world. Go back and crawl on your knees to him!" "His will be done!" "No! My will be done! Earth is mine! That was the deal!" "For three years and some days more."

"Not if I can help it."

"You cannot."

"No? Look at the earth. It is cinder, and my throne sits in the holy mountain!"

"If you look upon it. You will find that has not come about."

Michael conjured a vision of the missiles splashing harmlessly into the sea and all seven volcanoes sleeping quietly. "Seems you can't even trust demons these days!'

"My Demons? They have betrayed me.

"Seems you sent then to the harpies once too often."

"I hate you! You are nothing! You even bow down to man!" "If it pleases God!"

"Well, it doesn't please me!" The Red Dragon transformed into a Roman soldier dressed in full armor. Beneath the armor was a red tunic and on his head was a helmet on which was an Imperial crest. In his right hand was a sword, and in his left a dagger. "Now get the hell off my earth or die here and now!"

"Lucifer, will you ever clean up your act?"

"Come on! A rematch! On my turf! Now!"

"Soon, perhaps."

"I forgot! You must beg him for permission. Something I never did!"

"I regret that for all the agony it has cost the world."

"I have a better idea. Ask the Nazarene to come. Just me and him to settle it once and for all!"

"Are you sure you want that?"

"May I be damned – if I lie!"

"I think he will find that amusing." Michael chuckled.

Lucifer did not laugh. "Go back and grovel, Michael. I will be here, my sword at the ready if you ever get the courage to end this!"

Michael put his hand on his sword handle and was tempted to pull it.

"Do it, Michael! Just you and me! Use your free will and do as it commands you!"

Michael took his hand off the handle of the sword. "My will works for my selfish desires. His will works for the good of all!"

"Well I will be waiting on the plain of Esdraelon if you are any of the heavenly hosts have the courage to come face me. Let's get it on and end it now! "Satan vanished in a fit of rage.

Michael vanished moments later, leaving Sam alone, shivering with wonder and doubt.

Sam psyche was woozy from the avalanche of illusion that had assailed his senses. He felt rabid cynicism begin to seep back into his spirit until he looked at the bone whistle, he held in one hand and the piece of wormwood he held in the other. He put both in his pockets and shuddered with loneliness for Tiye. Yet, he hesitated to go after her. There was some doubt about her, but there was more forgiveness and love in his heart. After all, who was he to judge? Had he not once been among the greatest of sinners? He was trying to decide what to do when Tiye appeared out of the shadows.

Sam looked at Tiye and held out his fingers for her touch.

Tiye smiled and touched her fingertips to his.

Their eyes met in perfect love.

Sam smiled as he took her into his arms. They held each other for a long moment before they shared a sweet kiss. When the kiss was broken, they both looked around to see they were standing on top of Tissasack overlooking Tenaya Canyon.

"That was some ordeal." Sam sighed.

"What was?"

"You know the Tree, the Book, and all that celestial stuff."

"What are you talking about?"

"The Book? The seals? You were about to open…" Sam stopped.

Tiye looked puzzled a moment. "Sam, I just broke free of the Goons guarding me in the Control room!"

Sam was stunned for a long moment as he studied her eyes. "You weren't in a hologram with me at the altar before the Book of Life?"

"Yes. It was my deception for Malcolm."

"I mean after that. The real one?"

"Sam, I was in the Control room infecting his systems to free John and his Keepers."

"The control room. How did you get past the Goons?"

"Seems Eric and Oskar wanted a little payback."

"Then who was there with me?" Sam stopped and looked dead serious. "Let me see your heel!"

"What?"

Sam got to his knees and looked at her right heel. He gritted his teeth when he saw the implant on her right heel, then got back up and glared at her. "Why aren't you in pain?"

Tiye stepped back and looked offended. "What are you accusing me of?"

"I don't know. You are implanted!"

"Yes."

"You admit it! Damn, woman! When will the betrayal stop?" Sam grabbed her by the arms and shook her.

Tiye broke his hold and stepped back. "The implants are powerless now. I saw to it, and he cannot reboot them. None of his programs will work anymore. Soon, all his systems will be down – forever! Okay?" Tiye snapped at him.

Sam looked at her with doubt, then reluctant admiration. "That was your plan all along?"

"Yes! I created the monster. My atonement was to destroy him."

"Well done."

"No, thanks to you."

Sam had to nod in slow agreement. "He's going to be awfully pissed."

"Very angry indeed. But his Holocasts will now reveal his true self to the world, and he is going to be busy taking revenge on the Demons who failed him."

"And The Keepers?"

"Their free will has been restored."

"Let's pray they use it wisely."

"Amen."

They fell quiet as they heard singing on the wind echoing from inside the Holy Mountain.

"Just a closer walk with thee. Please, my savior, let it be…" The Keepers sang God's praise.

As Sam listened, his doubt turned to admiration, although he still was uncertain who to trust and what exactly to believe.

Tiye looked sad before she turned and walked away.

Sam started to call after her but thought it better to let her be for a time. For now, he would go to Pywiack and take a long cleansing shower, then go to her and beg her forgiveness.

CHAPTER TWENTY-SIX

JUDGMENT DAY EVE

Michael gripped the handle of the Sword of the Word. Gabriel put his hand on Michael's sword hand. "No, Michael!"

"Yes, it's past time – it was ended!"

"You are letting him bait you into disobedience!"

"No, I have permission to be at the ready with him this day."

"You mean the time has come?"

"That is not a certainty, but I am told to stand upon Megiddo and wait."

Gabriel picked up the horn.

Michael motioned for him to put it down. "Watch and wait."

Gabriel nodded and laid the trumpet down.

* * *

The plain of Esdraelon, beneath Mt. Megiddo in northern Israel, is close to the Kishon River on the southern edge of the south of Haifa, where Mount Carmel can be seen in the distance. It is here that the battle of Armageddon was to be fought in God's time.

Lucifer hoped to upset that timing. He grinned as he stood atop Mt. Carmel and conjured a vision of the world he now claimed as his own. Taking each country in turn, he showed the Godless debauchery that the world had become. The few churches still standing were empty of worshipers who could be found at gaming tables, liquor stores, or Drug Fests. Satanic rituals were held before each public event and were mandatory in every school. Lawlessness prevailed throughout the world as Police forces were dissolved, and no private gun ownership was allowed. All communities were ruled by self-righteous Commissars who exempted themselves from irrational rules enacted behind heavily guarded havens. Vast reaches of territory were empty of children's laughter, for few were allowed to be born.

The maddening cries of rape, revelry, and rioting drowned out any rational discourse. The din of evil covered the world, and the prayers of the few devout people of God could not be heard.

"Look upon it, Nazarene. It is too late for you. They cannot be redeemed. There is naught but my servants in all the corners of the earth. I have established my kingdom here. Here you are not wanted." His voice echoed across the empty plain as he stood holding his sword and dagger at the ready. "Come on! I'm ready! Let's do it!" Lucifer's voice thundered.

There was no echo as darkness enveloped the plain.

"Always your conditions and time, right? Okay? I didn't expect a fair fight." Lucifer scoffed.

His reply was a ray of celestial light that flooded the plain. The light blinded Lucifer for a moment. When he could see clearly again, he saw a man in a humble carpenter's dress carrying a carpenter's toolbox, standing 33 yards away.

"You come in a mortal dress with but the tools of a simple Carpenter?" Lucifer cackled.

The Carpenter nodded.

Lucifer waved his sword, and from all sides of the plain came the thunder of hoofbeats. Not the rhythmic sound of horses but an arrhythmic, frightening sound of huge cloven hoofs pounding the earth. They were followed by horrible creatures astride, even terrifying ogres, and led by a massive dragon with seven heads and ten huge, sharp horns. There were Horsemen as serpents with a hundred heads; Horsemen with the bodies of lions and the heads of leopards; horsemen of grotesque shapes that resembled nothing known to creation.

Michael stepped up and started to draw his sword.

The Carpenter motioned for him to put it away.

Michael reluctantly sheathed it and stepped back.

Lucifer commanded his legions forward. They came toward The Carpenter with unrelenting ferocity. When they were almost upon him, The Carpenter took an Adz from his toolbox. When he held the Adz up to the light, it cast the shadow of a cross, and the beasts vanished yelping in agony.

Lucifer snarled in anger and motioned with his hands, and a hail of bloodstone and fire poured down upon the plain, and the sun seemed to fall from the sky. He sent Giant scorpions and satyrs with fiery swords at The Carpenter.

The Carpenter raised the Adz again and sent them to oblivion.

Lucifer could barely disguise his frustration. Then he smiled and morphed into The Angel of Light, assuming a form so beautiful it would blind mortal man.

It did not impress The Carpenter.

"Am I not the most beautiful thing in the creation?" Lucifer said. "Look upon me! Come join me, and we will share the throne together!"

The Carpenter held up the Adz so that the shadow of the cross fell on Lucifer. In an instant, all the light drained away from Lucifer, and he stood inside his Temple with the walls crashing around him. All he had made was crumbling before him.

The Keepers were gone and the Pews were filled with hideous Demons and desperate souls weeping and gnashing their teeth.

Michael looked upon him with pity before he and The Carpenter vanished leaving Lucifer alone.

Lucifer fell to his knees from the weight of impending doom. As he did, he felt the urge to cry. A feeling he had never felt before. He shook it off, got to his feet and began to prepare new levels of hell for the Demons who had betrayed him. Then he would return to the Holy Mountain and work on a perfect plan. He knew it was still possible to save himself if he avoided his earlier mistakes.

For the people of the earth still slept.

CHAPTER TWENTY-SEVEN

Tiye and Sam stood alone beside his mother's grave in a secret part of Tenaya Canyon.

Tiye ran her fingers through his hair which was now darker and devoid of curls. His cheekbones were more prominent, and he had the golden skin of an Ahwahnee warrior. "I think you are home, my love."

"Yes, no matter where I traveled in the world, I was always happiest at Pywiack."

Tiye looked at his neck missing the necklace with the Golden Acorn.

"I'm sorry you lost it, Sam." Tiye seemed genuinely sympathetic.

"Not lost. I'll find it."

"Your mother made it for you?"

"It was passed down."

"From Tenaya?"

"That's the myth."

"Well, it was beautiful." Tiye paused and looked at the sadness in his eyes. "Are you okay?"

"Now that I know who I am?"

Tiye nodded.

Sam reached out to her with his fingers. They touched their fingertips and smiled. He took her in his arms and kissed her gently. "Yes, my love. For the first time in my life, I know what happiness is."

Ahwahnee was devoid of Malcolm's machines or any sign he had ever done anything to it. Both their memories were cloudy, and neither could have told you if minutes or years had passed or what had happened yesterday.

"I'm glad you quit, Mabius Media, Sam." Tiye offered.

"I should have quit long ago," Sam replied.

"Can I ask what the breaking point was?"

Sam looked over the beauty of the valley. "He wants to put up condos here in Yosemite."

"Like the ones at Yellowstone?"

"Yeah!" Sam smiled and looked at her with affection mixed with curiosity.

"Okay, what's on that suspicious mind of yours?" Tiye quizzed.

"Me? Suspicious of what?"

"You are wondering about him and me."

"He does have this thing about you."

"Malcolm and I go way back. I must admit I set him up. He was a nice guy then and was generous with financing my projects!"

"I know…"

"Don't ask about Donavan and anything else – because you are no saint!"

"Hey! I was just…."

"Just looking at me with those accusatory eyes!"

"I'm sorry." Sam paused to look serious for a moment. "Can I ask about this thing he has calling you, Queen Lillith?"

Tiye shot Sam an angry look, then grinned. "You suspect me of being a Demon, Sam?"

"No! Oh? No! No! No!"

"So why are we talking about this?"

"It's just that the last thing he asked, as I walked out of his office, was to take care of Queen Lillith for him."

"Will you believe me if I answer that?"

"Yes! Yes, of course."

"I have no idea!" Tiye insisted with a firm look that told Sam no more questions were allowed.

Sam reached for her hand. She held back, then held out her fingertips.

Sam looked puzzled.

"Touch yours to mine."

"What?"

"Come on. Let our fingertips touch."

Sam scoffed a moment, then put his fingertips to hers. He smiled when he felt the pleasant tingle of true love. He smiled at her, broke the touch. Their eyes met in quiet understanding, then took her in his arms and they shared a tender kiss. When they broke the kiss they embraced and sat quietly for a long time, watching the mystical serenity, and cleansing power of Pywiack's waters, the glory of Tuolumne meadows, and the pristine skies of the Ahwahnee Eden.

Sam stood up and looked around, savoring the views.

Tiye noticed her purse was partially open, and the necklace with the Golden Acorn could be seen inside. She grabbed the purse and eased it closed. "So, what will you do now?" Tiye asked as she sighed in relief.

Sam thought it over for a moment. "I've applied to teach at Sac State."

"You can live on an Assistant Geology Professor's salary?"

Sam took her hand and pulled her close. "What about a combined income?"

"Is that a proposal?"

"Will you?"

"Will, I what?"

"You know."

"No! Tell me."

"You're going to make me spell it out?"

"You bet, Buster!"

Sam thought it over. He looked deep into her eyes and smiled. "Will you...Marry...me?"

Tiye thought it over and shook her head. "I promised my parents I would marry in my faith."

"You haven't been to the temple in years!"

"Meaning what?"

"You told everyone in comparative religion class you were agnostic."

"Yes, but not an atheist!"

"Ok? I take it back, for God's sake."

"Your proposal?"

"Yes."

"I consider it on hold."

Sam looked a little disappointed, shrugged and changed the subject. "What do you think of all this end times talk?"

"Nothing that hasn't been said since the beginning of time." There was a crack of lightning from a clear blue sky followed by a loud series of thunderclaps. In the distance descending from the clouds and coming at them was a man on a white horse. As it thundered by them, Sam and Tiye ducked. They watched in awe as it faded into a misty heaven that glowed with a golden hue.

"A hologram of Malcolm's?" Sam asked.

"He is running an end times program." Tiye thought it over.

"But no pixel bleed."

"Meaning?"

"Hamlet, act one, scene five."

"There are more things in heaven and earth…"

"…Than are thought of in your philosophy." Tiye finished and looked at Sam. "So not so cynical anymore, Sam?"

"I met this preacher who is trying to save me from myself."

"John Pattos?"

"Yeah. A defrocked priest and a real holy Joe. You know him?"

"Yes. He is asking for me to develop some Podcasts and wants some broadcast time on my network."

"Anyway, he has me reading the book of Revelations."

"That's hard to understand, isn't it?"

"Not really."

"Oh, you figured out what serious biblical scholars have spent their lives trying to understand."

"Yep!"

"Well Mister theologian Summa Cum Laude, please regale me with your wisdom."

"You really want to know?"

"Oh, yes. Stop the presses!"

"Forget it."

"No, come on. Let's have it."

Sam waited until he saw the cynicism fade from her eyes. "Jesus wins."

END

"Therefore, stay awake, for you do not know on what day your Lord is coming. But know this, that if the master of the house had known in what part of the night the thief was coming, he would have stayed awake and would not have let his house be broken into. Therefore, you also must be ready, for the Son of Man is coming at an hour you do not expect."

—MATTHEW 24:42-44